WHAT IF?

WHAT IF?

Religious Themes in Science Fiction

MIKE ALSFORD

DARTON·LONGMAN+TODD

For my Father, who first gave me an appreciation of
science fiction
And for my Mother, my Sister,
Sally, and Sorren who gave me everything else.

First published in 2000 by
Darton, Longman and Todd Ltd
1 Spencer Court
140–142 Wandsworth High Street
London SW18 4JJ

ISBN 0–232–52347–9

A catalogue record for this book is available from the British Library.

Designed by Sandie Boccacci
Phototypeset in 9³/₄/13³/₄pt Trump Medieval by Intype London Ltd
Printed and bound in Great Britain by
Page Bros, Norwich, Norfolk

Contents

Preface

Since the early part of the 1990s I have been teaching an undergraduate course entitled 'Religious Themes in Future Fiction'. Originally this course was designed for final year theology students but increasingly it began to attract students of philosophy, literature, history, politics and sociology until finally there were as many non-theologians as theologians. In many instances the students attending the course had no prior interest in the genre of science fiction – or, as I prefer to call it, future fiction – nor did they necessarily possess any particular interest in organised religion. What I have discovered over the years is that students are intrigued by this course largely because of the space it creates in which to discuss and examine ultimate or primal issues relating to human existence – issues that are and have always been staple to the religious and philosophical diet – from a unique perspective.

What is perhaps even more interesting is the fact that while those not involved in academia or full-time education often balk at discussing, for example, theories of knowledge and human nature per se – feeling themselves theoretically ill-equipped to engage with these difficult subjects areas – these same people will happily discuss why the android 'Data' in *Star Trek* ought properly to be considered human and why living in the virtual, illusory world of *The Matrix* is to be rejected, no matter how pleasant, on the grounds of it being 'unreal'. The genre of SF, it seems to me, has the capacity to permit everyone, irrespective of their educational background, access to debates, discussions and speculation about some of the biggest questions that concern the human race.

The SF critic Robert Scholes has this to say of the genre that he calls 'fabulation':

Fabulation, then, is fiction that offers us a world clearly and radically discontinuous from the one we know, yet returns to confront that known world in some cognitive way. Traditionally, it has been a favorite vehicle for religious thinkers, precisely because religions have insisted that there is more to the world than meets the eye, that the common-sense view of reality – 'realism' – is incomplete and therefore false. Science, of course, has been telling us much the same thing for several hundred years. The world we see and hear and feel – 'reality' itself – is a fiction of our senses, and dependent on their focal ability, as the simplest microscope will easily demonstrate. Thus it is not surprising that what we call 'science' fiction should employ the same narrative vehicle as the religious fictions of our past. In a sense, they are fellow travellers.[1]

The genre of science fiction in its literary and cinematic forms serves to stimulate explorations into the unknown, to raise questions about human nature and destiny which then prompt further investigations into the theological and philosophical traditions that have grappled with these issues since the disciplines began. The genre acts as a meeting point where students from a range of academic discourses – and indeed those with no formal academic background – may engage with primal issues and share insights drawn from their own areas of expertise and their own lived experience.

This book is a direct result of both my undergraduate teaching and years spent discussing science fiction themes and ideas with anyone who would join in. For this reason I owe all the students who have contributed so enthusiastically to my course, and all those others who have discussed a much-loved genre with me in more informal settings, a debt of thanks for they have helped to define the scope of this present work, what it is as well as what it is not.

I
'Aliens and Androids and Cyborgs, Oh My!'

What we shall do and what we shall not do in this book

There is an ancient theological method which, upon recognising the essential mystery surrounding the being of God and the attendant inadequacy of human speech about such a God, proceeds by first establishing what God is *not*. This '*via negativa*', while clearly of limited value, often seems to me to be a good place to start all manner of intellectual exercises. Setting the boundaries of one's exploration and identifying the limits of one's interest and, indeed, one's reach are important first steps for any study, particularly one which deals both with religion and with a genre that boasts such an enthusiastic and well-informed following as does science fiction.

There are many excellent histories of the genre of science fiction which seek to establish the origins of this unique literary form and to trace its development through novel, short story and film.[1] This, however, is not one of them. There are also, albeit far fewer, attempts at identifying specific Christian motifs within the genre: messianic imagery, Christian symbolism and ideology, for example.[2] This book does not pretend to accomplish this in any direct way either. The intention here is to try to create a sense of interdisciplinary exploratory space as a context for engaging with primal issues relating to human nature and destiny. It is not the intention of the book to argue that the genre of science fiction is the only resource for creating such a space – merely that it is a valuable one and that it provides a unique perspective that less speculative fictions are hard-pressed to furnish. While my own religious expertise resides firmly within the Judaeo-Christian tradition, and thus many if not all of my specifically religious examples, comments and observations are drawn from that source, nevertheless this is not a book of Christian theology. In exploring what I have referred to as primal themes we have to do here with the fundamental questions to which religion claims to have an answer: Who are we? What is our destiny? Why is it so? – the infamous who?, what? and why? questions.

The intention here is to allow the genre to raise questions and make suggestions, to provoke and stimulate so that we might encounter the primal themes for the first time or engage with them in a new way. Science fiction has an unrivalled ability to provide this service by virtue of its inherent flexibility, its indeterminate character as speculative fiction, its ability to go beyond what is and to ask 'what if?'. Writers of science fiction delight in asking old questions in new ways, by altering the context of the question, by asking it in unfamiliar, sometimes disturbing ways. Often the science fiction writer is able to lull us into a false sense of security by creating an environment so apparently alien to our own that we do not recognise the immediate relevance of the issues being presented until they leap out and confront us from a myriad of different times and places.

The ability of human beings to indulge in exercises of self-transcendence, to look beyond themselves and their present context and to ask 'what if?' is both a blessing and a tragedy and science fiction exploits this tension to the full. To contemplate a destiny amongst the stars whilst at the same time recognising our capacity for greed and self-destruction; to aspire to new levels of existence, transformations to ever more blessed states of being, while acknowledging our equal potential to create and become monsters; to look forward to a future paradise or to dread the end results of urban decay and social collapse: hope and dread – these are indeed two of the poles that define us. The existentialist philosopher Martin Heidegger speaks of *Dasin*, the thrown-ness of being, our unnegotiated presence here and now which defines our present existence by binding us to a past and orientating us towards the future. It is only through an awareness of our historical 'situatedness' – with all that this entails in terms of our hopes and fears – that we can come to terms with our condition as human beings and seek an authentic mode of existence in the world in which we find ourselves.

In the pilot episode of the television series *Star Trek: Deep Space Nine* a human being, Ben Sisko, encounters a quasi-godlike alien species who exist outside of time. Much of the conversation between these two radically different life forms focuses on an attempt to explain human existence in terms of linear time. The aliens create a variety of scenarios from Sisko's past to facilitate his explanation of linear time. One is taken from his memory of a baseball game.

SISKO: *Every time you throw this ball a hundred different things can happen in the game. He might swing and miss, he might hit it, the point is, you never know. You try to anticipate, set a strategy for all the possibilities as best you can. But in the end, it all comes down to throwing one pitch after another and seeing what happens. With each new consequence, the game begins to take shape.*

ALIEN: *And you have no idea what that shape will be until it is completed?*

SISKO: *That's right. In fact, the game wouldn't be worth playing if we knew what was going to happen.*

ALIEN: *You value your ignorance of what is to come?*

SISKO: *That may be the most important thing to understand about humans. It is the unknown that defines our existence. We are constantly searching – not just for answers to our questions but also for new questions. We are explorers. We*

explore our lives day by day, and we explore the galaxy,
trying to expand the boundaries of our knowledge.[3]

Ironically it is the aliens who identify the root cause of Sisko's
own dysfunction – that he continues to exist in the past, at
the moment of his wife's death aboard a starship. The aliens
recreate the scene and confront Sisko with it.

SISKO: *(grief-stricken and angry) What is the point of bringing*
    me back again to this?
ALIEN: *We do not bring you here, you bring us here, you exist*
    here . . . None of your past experiences helped prepare you
    for this consequence.
SISKO: *And I never figured out how to live without her.*
ALIEN: *So you choose to live here. It is not linear.*
SISKO: *No, it's not linear.*

The theologian Wolfhart Pannenberg has gone to great lengths
to reassert the eschatological nature of the Christian religion
(that is, its concern with final destiny) and its accompanying
anthropology. Making extensive use of the work of the nineteenth-century philosopher G. F. W. Hegel, Pannenberg
deploys his notion of 'the ontological priority of the future' by
which he intends to convey the determining significance of
destiny for human existence and identity. Simply put, Pannenberg's argument is that we are beings in process, that what we
are *at present* is transitory and must continually give way to
that which we are to become in the future. Ultimately, our
being and identity can only come into true focus at the end of
the process of becoming, in the same way that a story is only
completely revealed once it has been told. Orientation towards
the future is for Pannenberg both a defining characteristic of
human being and an indication that we may define ourselves
only by looking beyond ourselves. This truth, argues Pannenberg, is fundamental to a religious understanding of human
existence.

For me, one of the most compelling reasons for a theological
consideration of science fiction is that it concerns itself with

issues that lie at the very heart of the theological enterprise, questions concerning the identity, origin and destiny of the human species. While there are indeed specific works within the genre which seek to address religion as such, we should not limit ourselves simply to these. It is the broader arena of the human condition in general that forms the common ground between theology and science fiction.

Since the nineteenth century much of the focus for contemporary theological inquiry has been on the human question. Theologians from Schleiermacher to Pannenberg have adopted an immanent methodology (seeing God as pervading the whole of life) which seeks to address religious questions from the side of humanity. Prior to this John Calvin, a theologian who clearly wished to place God at the centre of his theology, began his *Institutes* with the statement: 'Without knowledge of self there is no knowledge of God.'[4]

Science – or, as I would rather say, 'Future' – fiction seeks to facilitate this knowledge of self by confronting us with that which we hope for and that which we dread, by creating situations in which none of our past experiences may help prepare us for the consequences.

The Enlightenment and the origins of Science Fiction

While I have tried to make it clear that I am not concerned to rehearse the history of the genre of science fiction here, it is none the less necessary to give some background information in order to help orientate the reader, particularly those for whom the genre is literally a closed book. I am fully aware of the various debates that have been conducted by literary theorists specialising in the field concerning the origins of the genre and what qualifies as a piece of science fiction and I do not intend to get embroiled in these discussions here. For the purposes of this work I shall restrict myself to a general and, in the main, uncontentious presentation of the contours of the genre, some of the defining characteristics rather than a full-blown history.

Brian Aldiss, one of the most significant authors and commentators currently working within SF, argues that the genre ought properly to be understood as issuing out of the English Romantic Movement of the late-eighteenth and early-nineteenth centuries. Principally he has in mind Mary Wollstonecraft Shelley's proto-SF novel *Frankenstein: or The Modern Prometheus*, first published in 1818 and revised in 1831.

> ... *science fiction was born in the heart and crucible of the English Romantic movement in exile in Switzerland, when the wife of the poet Percy Bysshe Shelley wrote 'Frankenstein: or, The Modern Prometheus'* ... *elements of that novel are still being explored in fiction, because they are still of seminal interest to our technological society. I seek to show that those elements were combined as they were, when they were, because Shelley's generation was the first to enjoy that enlarged vision of time* ... *without which science fiction is perspectiveless, and less itself. The task is made all the more pleasant because much of the science fiction of the last century and of this is of perennial fascination. When it concerns itself not only with technological problems but with the affairs of man's inwardness (as does much of the best writing), then it can approach the permanence of myth.*[5]

Early SF is very much a product of the Enlightenment of the seventeenth and eighteenth centuries and its legacy is still apparent within a great deal of the genre's output, even as we enter a new millennium. While movements of thought and changes in world-view – what T. S. Kuhn famously referred to as 'paradigm shifts'[6] – are notoriously difficult to pin down and define exactly, it is important here to outline the principle themes associated with the period known as the Enlightenment, for it is out of this intellectual and cultural ferment that Shelley's creature was born and with it the literary form that came to be known as science fiction.

It is beyond doubt that the Enlightenment represents the most significant influence upon Western culture and thought

since the golden age of Greek philosophy dominated by Soc-
rates, Plato and Aristotle. The entire modernist world-view is
the Enlightenment's legacy to us. This is a view of reality
determined by the presuppositions and values of the Enlightenment – with its pursuit of objective truth, its confidence in
science and technology, its suspicion of those things, such as
religion, which defy empirical verification, and its dismissive
attitude towards the old, the traditional and the past in favour
of the new, the innovative and the future. The Enlightenment
is responsible for creating the environment in which not only
modern science but the modern political landscape developed
through the work of thinkers such as John Locke, Thomas
Hobbes, John Stuart Mill, Jean Jacques Rousseau and Karl
Marx. The so-called human sciences such as psychology and
sociology, philosophical movements such as existentialism,
and ethical systems such as Jeremy Bentham's Utilitarianism,
were made possible and credible only in the contexts of the
radical disengagement with Christian metaphysics that the
Enlightenment represents.

So what then is the Enlightenment and how is it possible
that such a movement of thought could give rise to a whole
new literary genre? Although it is normally associated with
the eighteenth century, the so-called 'Age of Reason', the
Enlightenment can be seen as having its origins as far back as
the fifteenth century with the Renaissance and the Reformation, and to have continued to have an influence right into
the later part of the twentieth century.

The influx of intellectual stimulus into Western culture that
accompanied the fall of Byzantium in 1453 and the attendant
rediscovery of classical texts previously held in Eastern
libraries, coupled with the attack on church authority and the
emphasis upon the primacy of scripture initiated by Martin
Luther – the Renaissance and the Reformation respectively –
Western Europe found itself in a paradoxical position. On the
one hand these events served to reaffirm the long-held belief
in the superiority of the classics and the scriptures over any
contemporary products. The classics represented the achieve-

ments of a golden age of human civilisation, one that, it was hoped, would be reborn now that access to these texts was less problematic. The Bible, of course, was the Word of God, the primary authority in matters of life and faith, at least according to reformers such as Luther and Calvin. That the text of the Bible was to be made more readily available via expository preaching, commentaries and translations was a central motif within the work of all the major reformers. On the other hand, exposure to the classical works of philosophy and increased interest in issues of biblical interpretation stimulated by the Reformation provided the intellectual background necessary to *question* these very same traditional authorities. It was this reaction against authorities that would become a characteristic motif of the Enlightenment world-view.

The challenge to traditional authority structures took a number of related forms. First, there was the development of natural sciences and the experimental methodology that this enshrined. Next, there was the epistemological reorientation (epistemology concerns the theory of knowledge) towards the thinking subject as primary in the quest for clear and certain truth. Finally, but in some ways most significantly, there was the anthropological shift away from a view of humanity as contingent or dependent being and towards a view that understood human being as autonomous and independent.

While Copernicus was attempting to argue against a geocentric notion of the cosmos on the grounds of observation rather than dogmatic assertion, Francis Bacon was pioneering an experimental approach to the study of the world, one that might provide humanity with the tools necessary to engage in a systematic analysis of the natural world. Bacon argues that: 'Men have been kept back as by a kind of enchantment from progress in the sciences by reverence for authority, by the authority of men accounted great in philosophy, and then by general consent.'[7]

It was Bacon who coined the phrase 'knowledge is power'; that is to say, the power that the new scientific method would provide over the natural world would help to liberate humanity from the effects of the fall from grace described in the book of Genesis, restoring human sovereignty over nature. Bacon understood there to be two sources of knowledge, the Bible and nature, and whilst these are distinct they are nonetheless part of God's will and design as his word and work, respectively. Bacon was concerned with the acquisition of 'useful knowledge', knowledge that could be cashed-in in technological terms so that human existence might be improved and humanity's ills alleviated. Indeed, Bacon's agenda was clearly a theological one as he warns against two sources of error: (1) ignoring the will of God revealed in scripture; and (2) ignoring the power of God revealed in his creatures. Science is thus understood as a means toward the restoration of humanity's dominion over nature, something lost at the fall. Humanity, argues Bacon, 'fell at the same time from his state of innocency and from his dominion over creation. Both of these losses can even in this life be in part repaired: the former by religion and faith, the latter by arts and sciences.'[8]

Newton similarly regarded the true end of scientific activity as being 'the glory of the Creator and the relief of man's estate' and, while he certainly helped to develop a view of the natural world as a law-abiding machine, he nevertheless stopped short of defining it in terms of a self-sufficient one. The world may well obey a system of natural laws, however God is still intimately involved in the maintainence of that system. Newton's notion has been much criticised, notably by Leibniz.

The central epistemological shift which characterised the Enlightenment was the so-called 'turn to the subject'. This new philosophical orientation upon how and what 'I' know had its formal origins in the work of René Descartes who is said to have initiated the emphasis upon the thinking, rational self as the foundation for clear and certain truth, a foundation upon which modernism would subsequently construct a virtually deified notion of human reason. In his attempt to combat the scepticism that he saw as at least a possible outcome of the challenges increasingly faced by traditional authorities, Descartes deployed a method of 'systematic doubt'. By doubting all sources of knowledge that could not be known clearly and distinctly, Descartes concluded that the only thing that could be known in such a way is that one exists. This, he argues, is self-evidently so because no matter to what extent a person may be deceived by his senses, or even by some supposed malicious demon, there is still an 'I' who is being deceived, a conciousness that is aware of itself thinking. This conclusion is famously captured in the Latin phrase 'cogito, ergo sum' – 'I am thinking, therefore I am' – a view first argued for by the Christian theologian Augustine.

Descartes' other important contribution to the contours of modernity was the reintroduction into contemporary metaphysics of the mind/body dualism so prevalent in early Greek thought and so influential during the formative years of Christian theology. Descartes argues that there exist three distinct types of substance: God – that creative substance which orders and controls all that is; matter – the material world-machine, substance extended in space that is governed by divine law; and mind – thinking substance which is not part of the world-machine and is not extended in space. Physical bodies, argued Descartes, are little more than machines governed by natural law. In so far as they are merely physical entities, animals are nothing more than automata totally lacking in consciousness. Human beings, however, exist as a duality of body *plus* mind or spirit. Descartes' concern was to account for how mind and matter interact with each other: how is it that our thoughts affect our bodies? This proved to be a more difficult problem than Descartes first imagined and he settled on the rather unsatisfactory solution of arguing for the point of contact between mind and matter as existing in the pineal gland. This of course raises the question of what kind of substance this gland is.

What is interesting here, particularly with respect to the genre of SF, is the conception of essential human being as something which transcends the body. First of all Descartes' epistemology prioritises mind over matter, thought over physical substance, and secondly, his dualistic metaphysics establishes mind or spirit as that which is *essentially* human over and against our bodies which are merely animalistic machines. Descartes, along with the early natural scientists such as Bacon and Newton, still wished to preserve a place for God within their respective systems of thought: in Descartes' case this was to guarantee the accuracy of sense perception so that the physical world could be known at all and in Newton's it was to account for the stability of a natural order that threatened to collapse without transcendental intervention and which is in any event inherently contingent. The scene was nevertheless set for a full-blown naturalistic interpretation of reality that no longer required the hypothesis of God.[9]

It was John Locke who attempted to produce an epistemology that was founded upon sense perception alone and who denied the sort of innate knowledge of God deployed by Descartes. Locke famously argues that the human mind is, in the first instance, a *tabula rasa*, a blank slate which is subsequently written on by sense experience. In many ways this view opened up the way for a variety of social reforms as it suggested a view of the human condition that was not predetermined by any kind of divine or even naturally occurring human essence. Thus, a person is not born good or bad, intelligent or ignorant, inferior or superior, but becomes so as they are constituted by a range of experiences; nurture rather than nature becomes central to the notion of human identity. Education, social engineering and of course the natural sciences subsequently became the tools for the construction of a new utopian world order – indeed both the United States of America and the former Soviet Russia could be regarded as modernist social experiments of this kind. Humanity no longer ought to be understood as the bearers of some divine image or, more importantly, handicapped by any notion of original sin which establishes human being as essentially dysfunctional. Indeed, while Locke himself certainly saw humanity as being dependent upon God, particularly with respect to ethics, he was none-the-less a political revolutionary, arguing against the divine right of kings and the whole notion of hereditary power.[10] It was Locke who formulated the understanding of civil government being founded upon a social contract, a political ideal that has had a profound effect upon the British and American constitutions and, through Voltaire, upon revolutionary France. Government is thus seen to be based upon natural principles rather than metaphysical dogma.

If there is one philosopher who could be said to represent the spirit of the Enlightenment more than any other then that thinker would have to be Immanuel Kant. In his most famous work, the *Critique of Pure Reason*, Kant seeks to establish confidence in the capacity of human reason via a careful definition of its limits. In essence Kant maintains, following Locke, that all true knowledge is dependent upon sense experience but, he continues, it is the categories of thought – that is, the operation of human reason – which order these experiences into a meaningful perception of reality. Sense experience on its own is not enough to give us a world to live in, it is only once the raw data has been processed by human reason that we actually experience what we call the natural world.

It is the thinking subject, Descartes' 'cogito', that establishes its own reality in Kantian thought, not by virtue of creating an actual physical world, for Kant insists on maintaining the existence of a real world that is external to us, but by the application of the categories of the mind to establishing what we know as 'nature' or the 'natural order'. The Kant scholar L. W. Beck has this to say on the matter:

It was Prometheus who seized the prerogative of the gods and gave it to humankind. Through possession of fire, everything else could be created ... Man is no god, but in his creativity he may be godlike, and many of the tasks previously assigned to god in the creation and governance of the world are reassigned by Kant to man.[11]

It has been said that the ultimate question being addressed in all of Kant's work is 'What is man?' Beck claims, quite rightly I believe, that his final answer, typified in the *First Critique*, is 'man is creator'. In the first edition of the *Critique of Pure Reason* Kant expounds an understanding of man as the creator of his world by the operation of the categories of understanding upon the chaotic profusion of sense experience.

> ... *the order and regularity in the appearances, which we entitle nature, we ourselves introduce. We could never find them in appearances, had not we ourselves, or the nature of our mind, originally set them there. For this unity of nature has to be a necessary one, that is, has to be an a priori certain unity of the connection of appearances; and such synthetic unity could not be established a priori if there were not subjective grounds of such unity contained a priori in the original cognitive powers of our mind, and if these subjective conditions, inasmuch as they are the grounds of the possibility of knowing any object whatsoever in experience, were not at the same time objectively valid.*[12]

While sense experience provides us with a collection of chaotic forms, only the human understanding can provide the rules necessary for a unified view of reality. These rules, says Kant, are by no means external to us, being the *a priori* product of our understanding. 'They are not borrowed from experience; on the contrary, they have to confer upon appearance their conformity to law, and so to make experience possible.'[13] Indeed this whole line of argument within the *Critique of Pure Reason* might well be seen as the Kantian equivalent to a creation narrative, where epistemological order is established out of the chaos of sense perception.

Kant famously argues that as the categories of thought are capable only of ordering sense experience into meaningful knowledge, then it follows that all metaphysical speculation, because it claims to obtain data that transcends the senses, is invalid as true knowledge. Thus a sizeable proportion of philosophical discourse and practically all of the religious and theological debate was at a stroke rendered insignificant with respect to the acquisition of knowledge. Indeed, Kant considered metaphysical and theological reflection as a positive hindrance to the pursuit of knowledge as their conclusions were ultimately beyond empirical verification and they thus diverted attention away from more fruitful areas of thought.

In the wake of the burgeoning confidence in the modernist world-view with its secular outlook, coupled with the devastating atheist critique of religion mounted by Ludwig Feurbach, Christian theology found itself at a critical juncture. In the main there have been three strategies deployed by theologians in an attempt to respond to modernism's apparent antagonism towards religion in general and Christianity in particular. The first, characterised by nineteenth-century liberal theologians such as Albrecht Ritschl and Adolf von Harnack, is to accommodate to the new world-view by seeking to recast religion in a largely naturalistic and ethical form. The second approach, typified by the Protestant theologian Karl Barth, seeks to immunise Christianity from the onslaughts of the Enlightenment by deploying a form of idealistic metaphysics that might only be engaged with by the faithful and then only at the initiative of God. Finally, the third approach, championed by the theologian Wolfhart Pannenberg, is to confront the Enlightenment world-view as simply that, an alternative view of reality that is itself open to critique, particularly in the light of its ability to provide satisfying answers to anthropological questions.

A great deal more could be said about the Enlightenment, its themes and its thinkers, but I believe enough has been said to support the view that a great deal of the most significant early works in SF deal with traditional Enlightenment issues: knowledge as power; optimism and suspicion as regards the new scientific method; the challenging of traditional limits and taboos; questions concerning human nature, knowledge and morality; and above all the notion of humanity as the creator of its own identity and indeed of its own world. Furthermore, with its emphasis upon human perception as the source of all true knowledge, questions concerning the reality of reality are raised by the Enlightenment. Is reality a fixed external 'something' that we experience, or do we, as Kant may be seen as suggesting in spite of himself, determine the shape of reality? If what is real is simply what my mind chooses to interpret and represent as such, then why should we not alter our perception of reality either chemically or electronically to suit our own tastes?

In the 1999 film *The Matrix* we are presented with a world in which humanity is dominated by intelligent machines who harvest human beings as raw material. In order to keep the human population subdued and compliant, and to incarcerate them efficiently, the machines have created the Matrix, a computer-generated artificial reality in which all of humanity perceive themselves to live out their lives. In the ordinary course of events data is taken in via our five senses and this data is then transmitted to the brain where it is ordered and interpreted into a perceived world. The Matrix bypasses the senses and transmits the data directly to the brain, which goes about its usual business of creating a representation of the world based upon the received data. To all intents and purposes humans understand themselves as existing in an ordinary world where they live and move and have their being, but in 'reality' they are suspended in nutrient tanks, their brains hooked up to the Matrix. In an interesting scene, a human being who has become aware of the nature of the Matrix and has been freed from it decides that the real world is actually rather bleak and uncomfortable in comparison to the reality provided within the Matrix. He reasons that, while he knows that the good food he is eating and the friends he has and the position of power that he occupies are all products of a sophisticated computer-generated virtual reality, does it really matter? If they feel real, if he actually experiences them as real, then they are real. How many people living within our own society would welcome such an option, I wonder?

The Enlightenment stimulated a whole range of questions that previously admitted to only dogmatic answers. In so doing it eventually, according to many post-modern theorists, established its own set of dogmatic responses. Nevertheless it did establish questions concerning human nature, identity and destiny, alongside those relating to ontology (a study of the nature of being), epistemology (the theory of knowledge) and ethics, as genuine questions worthy of exploration. It is for this reason that SF ought properly to be seen both as a product of the Enlightenment, in that it seeks to engage with these questions, but also as transcending the Enlightenment, in that it is the questions themselves that are central rather than any ensuing dogma.

What we find in the likes of Mary Shelley, Jules Verne and H. G. Wells, for example, is typical of this anxiety and fear coupled with an almost guilty revelling in the new technologies and in the potential for human creativity. In the H. G. Wells inspired film *Things to Come* the new scientific golden age is assaulted by an anti-scientific revolution, its leader crying out: 'What is this progress? What is the good of all this progress onward and onward? We demand a halt. We demand a rest . . . an end to progress!' Frankenstein has the scientific power to create life, to be as a god, he sneers at his reactionary teachers who, just as Bacon observed, hold back from making the major scientific advances through superstition and fear; and yet this is a horror story, not a celebration of human ingenuity. It poses the questions: Are there limits to the new science, both moral and functional? To what extent are we responsible for our creations? Will we be able to control what we have made? What is natural? Are we influenced by our creator or by our context? Is it nature or nurture that determines who we are? It is for this reason that it has been suggested that Shelley's Frankenstein be awarded the distinction of being regarded as the first true SF novel. This may or may not be case – I personally am inclined to agree – but either way, the novel most certainly does give an indication of the characteristic concerns of the genre, a genre that operates at the boundaries of world-views. It is for this reason that I favour the terms 'speculative' or 'future fiction' over the more traditional science fiction for this unique literary form.

Science and science fiction

The genre's interest in science and techology is, to a large extent, accidental in that its primary concern is always with human beings on the threshold of a paradigm shift, of a new way of conceiving of themselves and the world that they inhabit. The modernist shift was a movement away from the metaphysical, the spiritual and supernatural and towards the physical, material and natural, thus speculative or future fictions focused their attention upon issues relating to humanity's utilisation of technology and its long-term effects upon the human condition. As new insights were gained into the natural world and new tools were produced to permit us greater control over it, SF writers explored the hopes and fears bound up in these new technologies. Electricity, transistors, nuclear energy, microchips and genetic engineering – no sooner were these marvels of the modern age suggested by the scientific community than writers of SF gave us stories about electrically galvanised monsters, nuclear-powered submarines and spaceships exploring the cosmos, weapons of mass destruction, smart machines and superhumans. A good example of this is the much celebrated account of an incident in 1944 when the well-known SF magazine *Astounding*, edited by John W. Campbell, was investigated by US military intelligence. What prompted this interest by American intelligence agents was the observed similarity between a recently published story – 'Deadline' by C. Cartmill, in which details relating to the building of an atomic bomb were speculated upon – and actual research being conducted by scientists on the highly secret Manhattan Project. The editor of the magazine was eventually able to convince the government agents that the story was a piece of speculative fiction based on information in the public domain.

Writers from Shelley, Verne and Wells, through Asimov, Heinlein and Vogt, to Gibson, Stephenson and Cadigan have, in their own way, speculated upon humanity at its various crossroads. Once we have harnessed nuclear power, where will we allow it to take us? Once we are able to create thinking machines, how will they affect our own sense of identity? And once we are able to recreate and re-engineer ourselves, who and what will we become? To a very large extent the science and technology per se are not important – how a clone can be grown is an issue for the biological sciences; what we do with that clone and how it recasts our sense of humanity is the concern of the SF writer.

Brian Aldiss once made the point that, 'Science fiction is no more written for scientists than ghost stories are written for ghosts. Most frequently, the scientific dressing clothes fantasy. And fantasies are as meaningful as science. The phantasms of technology now fittingly embody our hopes and anxieties.'[14] This is a sentiment that I find myself in full agreement with and one which is echoed in the work of SF critic Robert Scholes. Scholes also speaks of 'future' rather than 'science fiction' although he favours the term 'fabulation' over them both. In his book *Structural Fabulation*, Scholes seeks to provide an account of the nature of SF and its place within contemporary culture and literature.

In works of structural fabulation the tradition of speculative fiction is modified by an awareness of the nature of the universe as a system of systems, a structure of a structure, and the insights of the past century of science are accepted as fictional points of departure. Yet structural fabulation is neither scientific in its methods nor a substitute for actual science. It is a fictional exploration of human situations made perceptible by the implications of recent science. Its favourite themes involve the impact of developments or revelations derived from the human or physical sciences upon the people who must live with those revelations or developments.[15]

This having been said, there has always been a strong tradition, especially in the early works of SF, to put the emphasis firmly on the 'science' rather than the 'fiction'. This was clearly the case with the man to whom the very term 'science fiction' is attributed, Hugo Gernsback (1884–1967). Gernsback was the editor of a number of pulp magazines during the 1920s and 1930s – notably *Amazing Stories*, first published in April 1926 – and the term he used was the rather unwieldy *'scientifiction'*. Gernsback was interested in developing a literary genre that took the form of prediction, a map of technological advances founded upon current scientific developments. A man deeply fascinated by electricity and radio, Gernsback sought to publish material that provided scientific insights for the young and encouraged them to look forward to a future characterised by technological marvels. For Gernsback, SF stories may very well be 'amazing', however they had nonetheless to be credible. The future described by Gernsback was a possible one founded upon real science extrapolated; he had little time for flights of fancy, as this 1932 quote makes clear:

Many modern science fiction authors . . . do not hesitate to throw scientific plausibility overboard, and embark upon a policy of what I call scientific magic, in other words, science that is neither plausible nor possible. Indeed it overlaps the fairy tale, and often goes the fairy tale one better.[16]

The genre has thus, from its earliest manifestations, exhibited a polarisation between its relationship with science and technology on the one hand and its fictional and speculative character on the other. Brian Aldiss refers to these two poles as *thinking* and *dreaming* and both these approaches have their own unique strengths and are well represented within the SF community.

For an example of the speculative SF so abhorred by Gernsback, we need look no further than *Star Trek*, arguably the most popular SF product of the century. The creator of this successful series, Gene Roddenberry, had a vision of the future as characterised by 'science unbounded'. Here we see a science almost godlike in its capacity to manipulate nature; little if anything is beyond the possibilities of Roddenberry's vision of future technology. This almost transcendental view of science and technology, coupled with Roddenberry's optimistic humanism, is close to Enlightenment utopianism. In *Star Trek* Roddenberry created an immensely popular and rather comforting universe in which we encounter a humanity that has overcome its differences and now devotes itself to the higher concerns of civilisation. The science deployed in the various *Star Trek* series is little more than meaningless techno-babble designed to provide futuristic window-dressing for stories that concern themselves, in the main, with human ethical dilemmas. This portrayal of super-science calls to mind a famous comment made by Arthur C. Clarke – one of the most significant figures in the SF community: 'Any sufficiently advanced technology is indistinguishable from magic.'[17]

Star Trek technology does indeed resemble magic in its ability to coerce nature and to achieve the apparently miraculous. Artificial life, trips backwards and forwards in time, and a medical technology that does not stop short at raising the dead – these are common features of an average *Star Trek* story but they are seldom the focus of attention.

In contrast to the *Star Trek* universe, and I would argue more in keeping with the Gernsback model of SF, we might consider the development of the cyberpunk sub-genre which reached its evolved form during the 1980s with the Film *Blade Runner* (1981) and William Gibson's award-winning trilogy *Neuromancer* (1984), *Count Zero* (1986) and *Mona Lisa Overdrive* (1988). While Gibson's work is regarded as archetypal cyberpunk, the sub-genre can be seen as having its roots in novels such as Alfred Bester's *The Demolished Man* (1953) and *The Stars My Destination* (1956), as well as John Brunner's *The Shockwave Rider* (1975). A recent excellent example of cyberpunk cinema, in terms of style as well as content, is the 1999 movie *The Matrix*.

Cyberpunk can best be described as 'SF noire' – imagine a high-tech Raymond Chandler novel and you are almost there. Although at first glance cyberpunk stories give the impression of a radically alien future dominated by new technologies, in many ways they represent a return to the Gernsback model of probable science and probable future. Cyberpunk attempts to draw on a variety of elements already familiar within contemporary urban culture without over-stepping the bounds of possibility. The most popular themes explored by cyberpunk authors are those to do with urban decay, cultural pluralism, invasive technologies, multinational and corporate power structures and the increasing significance of a world-wide data network. Cyberpunk stories are seldom set in the far future and rarely 'off world'. These are very much stories about 'our world', the landmarks are familiar to us, albeit dirtier and darker. The technology, far from being the super-science of *Star Trek*, is based upon current cutting-edge scientific developments, made popular and introduced at street level. William Gibson once made the point that for him the primary characteristic of new technology is that it gets closer to the skin. What he means by this is that technology is becoming increasingly invasive: what was once seen in public places next moved into our living rooms, then became something we wore on our bodies and ultimately will become something that is implanted inside our bodies. The interface between technology and the human person is at the very centre of the cyberpunk sub-genre – hence its name.

Ridley Scott's classic film *Blade Runner*, loosely based on the novel *Do Androids Dream of Electric Sheep?* by Philip K. Dick, is widely recognised as one of the finest examples of cyberpunk cinema. The film focuses attention upon issues relating to human personhood and identity by way of a consideration of artificial life. In many ways it revisits the questions raised by Mary Shelley as she asks us to reflect upon Frankenstein's creature. The film tells the story of a group of escaped 'replicants' – artificial humans created as slave labour by a multinational corporation – as they seek to establish their own unique identities and as they confront the fact of their own mortality. As replicants are a potential threat to humanity they are designed to have a lifespan of only a few short years.

Prior to his death one of the replicants ascends to the top of the corporate headquarters of his creator, his god, to ask for more life: 'Can the creator repair what he has made?' To which his creator responds that he made him as well as he could. This scene ends with the creator being killed by his anguished creation who is enraged by the powerlessness of his god.

There are those who would argue that it is time that we too killed off our powerless gods, be they supernatural beings or simply the natural order, who designed us to live for a mere 70 or 80 years, who failed to provide us with adequate protection from damage and illness, and who prevent us from achieving our true potential. Evolution is regarded as a painfully slow and inadequate process for enhancing the human design when compared to the rate at which technology develops. The new gods of biogenetic engineering promise us a variety of enhanced physical and mental abilities, if not for us then for our children. Once again, technology is seen as getting closer and closer to the skin until finally it gets under it.

Cyberpunk technology is undoubtedly futuristic but it also clearly belongs to a probable future. Writers such as William Gibson, Neal Stephenson and Pat Cadigan portray such ideas as genetic engineering, artificial body parts, virtual worlds and cybernetic interfaces as everyday background. While we must speak of them as 'things to come', there is little doubt that they will indeed come, unlike the super-science of *Star Trek*, whose concern is less with the impact of technology and more with interpersonal relations.

The present in the future

SF, paradoxically, has always concerned itself with the present, with images and icons that are recognisable to us now. In trying to understand the present and the implications of the decisions we make in it, SF writers attempt to transcend the present, to look forward into possible futures that are the products of our present activities. These anticipations of the future permit us to reflect upon the present and our place in it, upon our decisions, attitudes and activities, and furthermore they help to provide us with a sense of responsibility towards the future.

An orientation towards the future, openness to that which is beyond us is, according to the Christian theologian Wolfhart Pannenberg, essential to what it means to be human and, moreover, it defines humanity as essentially religious. Exocentricity – openness – as opposed to egocentricity – closedness – marks humanity out as a species that does not contain its own answers within itself. Humanity is, as Schleiermacher put it, characterised by being dependent; we are contingent beings. Commenting on J. G. Herder, Pannenberg makes this point:

The image of God, which is impressed 'on the mind' of human beings, functions as a teleological concept and standard for their behaviour. It can exercise this function because the image of God represents the goal of human existence as such, in keeping with Herder's conviction that 'we are not yet men, but are daily becoming so.' Thus the image of God and the selfness or humanness of human beings belong together: 'religion and humanity' are intimately connected for Herder.'[18]

Pannenberg goes on to describe the person of Jesus Christ as an anticipation of human destiny, the presence of the future kingdom of God within human history.

If Jesus is the true man through his dedication to God's future, in his message of the nearness of God's Lordship, as well as through the anticipatory fulfilment of human destiny in his own person through his resurrection from the dead so that truly human life becomes possible through community with him, then that realisation towards which all human hopes are aimed is already fulfilled in him in an anticipatory way.[19]

The genre of SF at its best – and I recognise that there is as much banal material produced within this genre as within any other – seeks to explore the question of our destiny, what we shall or might become and how knowledge of our possible futures can affect our present sense of self. Many, if not all, time-travel stories seem to me to represent a desire to access both the past and the future in the hope that we might gain greater control over the present. We are constantly exhorted not to live in the past, to lay to rest the ghosts of the past and to look towards the future, to live our lives looking forward rather than backwards in the manner of Dickins' Miss Haversham. Time-travel stories such as H. G. Wells' *Time Machine*, published in 1895, and David Gerrold's *The Man Who Folded Himself* (1973) and films such as *The Terminator* (1984) provide us with fascinating insights into human temporality. We exist *in time* and everything we do is related to and continuous with our past and our future. We are, as Heidegger would put it, 'situated', we have a temporal presence. Ray Bradbury's classic short story 'A Sound of Thunder' tells of a future where time travel has become a major part of the tourist industry. One such tourist opts for a prehistoric vacation during which he accidently treads on a butterfly. On his return he finds his own time dramatically transformed as a result of the cumulative effect of his prehistoric mis-step. Jungian psycho-analysis, the I-Ching and modern chaos theory all, in their own ways, make the same point concerning our interconnectedness with each other and the rest of reality.

It is interesting to note that this theme of interconnectivity and temporal situatedness has been explored in a number of successful films that, while studiously trying to avoid being identified with SF, would require very little in the way of modification to make them so. Frank Capra's *It's a Wonderful Life* (1946) has a dispirited George Bailey saved from suicide, via angelic rather than technological intervention, by allowing him to live for a time as if he had no past, thus permitting him to see what the world would have been like without him. *Groundhog Day* (1993) has the male lead reliving the same day over and over until he gets it right and *Sliding Doors* (1997) tells two parallel stories about the same woman, one in which she catches a particular train at a particular time and one in which she misses it.

Of course, while SF is a genre with a unique interest in the future, it clearly and inescapably echoes the present context of its production. Depictions of the future are often extrapolations of the present rather than genuine predictions and this would account for how quickly an SF film can appear out of date with respect to its attempts to portray the 'style' of the future. It is particularly interesting to view/read SF produced in the past, which attempts to portray the look and feel of our own present. Fritz Lang's classic 1926 film *Metropolis* is a good example of this, presenting us with a very 1920s image of the future, as is the 1936 film *Things to Come*. In this later film spaceships are shot out of an enormous cannon and the future is seen as a return to a sort of Greek golden age – quite a common motif within SF – where togas and sandals are back in fashion.

SF is by no means a crystal ball. In its presentation of a range of possible futures it seeks to confront us with challenges to our present view of the world and of ourselves. Some writers see themselves as trying to prevent the future by showing us what may be if we continue as we are. Some, on the other hand, wish to help usher in a future in which the curses of a disappointed god and the intractability of blind nature are overcome and paradise is regained. To this end the genre, in all its forms, destroys and rebuilds our world, bends time and space, experiments with our genetic code, enslaves us to other races and them to us, builds machines that are smarter than we are, casts us, by turn, as gods and monsters, and places us at the centre of a glorious and enlightened federation and then again at the dark heart of a foul and despotic empire. And all the while the question is the same: *What are we?* SF writers are surely no more likely to be able to answer this question definitively than anyone else. What they do, however, is engage with it through another, more manageable question, one that is more susceptible to humanity's unique creative and imaginative powers: *What if?*

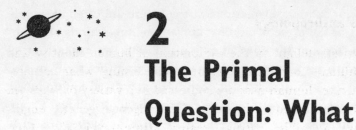

2
The Primal Question: What Are We?

I think it might be true to say that the fundamental questions that concern us are questions that concern US. No matter what field of research we are involved in, at the very root of human enquiry is the question concerning human nature. Thus we find the sciences and the arts in a never-ending quest to say something about human being. Theology too, despite its formal definition as God-talk, more often than not is concerned with **our** talk about God, **our** religious experience, the implications of belief in a God of a certain kind for **our** existence.

Science fiction, in most respects, is less to do with the future or technology than it is with the human condition. The question that consumes producers of SF as much as it does theologians and philosophers is what one might call the primal question: 'What are we?' In a very important way every alien story, every robot story, every BEM (bug-eyed-monster!) story, every end-of-the-world story and every time-travel story is concerned with this primal question to a greater or lesser degree. While we may indeed revel in the gadgetry of a possible future and the wonder of an alternative reality, it is the perspective on the human condition, cast into relief by imaginative variations in context, that proves to be most valuable.

SF as anthropology

SF writers delight in the exploration of human identity and the human condition. Questions concerning what actually constitutes human-ness are addressed in a variety of ways via stories concerned with artificial intelligence, genetic engineering, androids, virtual reality, time-travel and alien encounters.

In an episode of *Star Trek: The Next Generation* the android, Data, is put on trial to establish whether it/he has the rights of personhood or is simply property.[1] The ensuing debate inevitably revolves around the criteria for establishing personhood. The story is not in fact about an android on a spaceship but about what it means to be human. This is brought into focus when the android's defence council turns the question around and asks the court to define what it is that makes anyone a person. The film *Robocop* explores a similar question: what can be taken away from or for that matter added to a human being and still allow them to retain their humanity?

One of the best pieces of SF written over the last few years is Pat Cadigan's *Fools*[2] which explores the significance of memory for human identity. Cadigan presents us with a cyberpunk environment where memories are bought and sold like drugs and where consequently individual identity is a tenuous thing. Another story, by Philip K. Dick, *We can Remember it for you Wholesale*, released as the film *Total Recall*, covers much the same ground.

It is important to learn to read future fiction sensitively if one is to identify the concerns that lie behind the unusual scenarios. Films like *Forbidden Planet*, *The Terminator* and *Alien* are rich with insights into the human condition and are susceptible to a multiplicity of readings and interpretations. Similarly, novels such as *The Death Guard* (P. G. Chadwick) *The Ship Who Sang* (Ann Macaffrey) and Asimov's *Robot* series provide us with new ways of reflecting on war, our bodies and ethics.

In many ways the debates within SF concerning the nature of humanity echo those within the Christian tradition. Theologians have always struggled with the notion of humanness, whether it be in the context of trying to establish what exactly constitutes the 'image of God' or trying to understand the effects of sin on that 'image' – or within Christological debates, relating to the extent of Jesus' humanity. Does our humanness reside in our physicality, in our mental, moral or social capacity, in an indefinable something called a 'soul' or perhaps in our orientation and relationship to God?

These are primary theological questions and central to SF. As we have noted, a significant number of early SF stories focused upon the potential for science to create life. More often than not the offspring of science are depicted as soulless and thus by definition inhuman and immoral – such a definition being dependent upon a range of presuppositions about humanity and inhumanity. Latterly, interest has been expressed within the genre concerning the extent to which our bodies are important to our 'humanness'. This is particularly so within the cyberpunk sub-genre where questions are raised concerning the effect of increased amounts of cybernetic enhancement or prolonged involvement in a virtual reality upon our sense of human identity. Certainly within the Christian tradition, attitudes to the body have been ambiguous, to say the least, and this has had a profound effect upon the tradition's ability to speak sensitively to issues of sexuality for example.

Technology in SF thus functions as a literary device to engineer a set of experimental circumstances for human beings to explore. Many SF writers know little if any 'hard science' – that is not their concern, what they are concerned with principally is anthropology.

It would seem that many of the very earliest pieces of SF focused on the theme of human nature: Mary Shelley's *Frankenstein*, Robert Louis Stevenson's *The Strange case of Dr Jekyll and Mr Hyde* and H. G. Wells' *The Island of Dr Moreau* spring immediately to mind. In Mary Shelley's proto-science-fiction novel, first published in 1818, we encounter not so much a monster but rather ourselves, humanity. Are we nothing more than a collection of biological odds and ends? Are we any different in kind from Frankenstein's creature? Indeed, perhaps the only true monster present in Shelley's story is the human being who rejects and abandons his own creation, his offspring. Perhaps Shelley is, after all, telling us how monsters are made.

Another early example of SF's concern with the question of human nature can be seen in the 1915 German film entitled *Homunculus* (based on a novel by R. Reinert). This story concerned itself with a scientist's creation of an artificial man based on what can best be described as an enlightenment or rationalist template. This artificial life form was a soulless being devoid of all emotion, a man of pure reason. The premise of the story is that without a soul this new man inevitably becomes evil and establishes himself as a dictator with plans for world domination, thus undermining Enlightenment confidence that pure reason might lead to a better human society.

In 1918 fears concerning scientific manipulation of human procreation were aired in the film *Alraune* (based on a novel by Hans Heinz Ewers). The mad scientific experiment under examination here is artificial insemination, where the semen of a murderer is used to impregnate a prostitute. We might well ask, what possible chance could any offspring have? However, the surrogate father hoped to prove his theories concerning the environmental effects upon human character. The Enlightenment, in various ways, had sought to teach us that we are born as blank slates to be written on, we are neither good nor evil but have the potential to become either depending on our context. Edgar Rice Burroughs tells us of the infant Lord Greystoke, for example, who having been lost in the African jungle and brought up by apes becomes Tarzan the ape man despite his aristocratic blue blood. Nevertheless, in the film *Alraune* the product of this unholy alliance between science, immorality and violence is an evil, twisted woman, a woman, it should be noted, who delights in driving men to their destruction. The experiment is a failure and the view that what we are is determined via accident of birth, or perhaps by the will of the gods, is reaffirmed. It might be of interest to note that this film was remade in 1928 and released in Britain as *The Daughter of Destiny*. However, such was the sensitivity to the issue of artificial insemination that the film censors removed all reference to it, which made the film all but incomprehensible.

Early SF, not surprisingly, seems to have mixed feelings about our increasing ability to recreate and thus redefine what is truly human. While we can exult along with Victor Frankenstein – and all the mad scientists that followed in his footsteps – in the potential for science to take us beyond current orthodoxy and make us the masters of nature, still there is the fear of what we might unleash upon the world. It is by no means insignificant that Mary Shelley chose as the subtitle for her novel 'The Modern Prometheus'.

If the earliest SF set a kind of anthropological agenda for the genre, it would seem that contemporary SF has by no means tired of the basic question 'what are we?' Indeed this, as I have already said, may be seen as representing the primal human question not only for academia but for every human person.

Gene Roddenberry's *Star Trek*, clearly the most successful SF creation of the twentieth century, has developed in many different directions, from the 1960s classic series which first introduced the Starship Enterprise, the United Federation of Planets and of course Captain Kirk and Mr Spock, to the most recent spin-off *Star Trek Voyager*. One would be hard-pressed, I believe, to find more than a handful of *Star Trek* episodes from across all four series that did not address the question of human nature and identity in some form or another. Whether it be Captain Kirk debating morality with a mad computer, Captain Picard holding forth on the dubious nature of human genetic manipulation, Captain Sisko experiencing prophetic visions of alien gods or Captain Janeway arguing the merits of individuality with the Borg collective, the primary concern with humanness is ever apparent.

Similarly, Michael Straczynski's epic TV series *Babylon 5* from the 1990s, presents us with two opposing and ancient forces of light and darkness who, on encountering lesser species such as humanity, invariably ask the questions: 'who are you?' and 'what do you want?' It is remarkable just how difficult these two seemingly straightforward questions are to answer. To enquire into one's own identity is fraught with consequence and difficulty. If we are too specific we run the risk of limiting our potential; if we are not specific enough we are just as likely to lose any sense of focus and individual significance. I like to think of myself as a father because it provides a satisfying sense of order and meaning to my life, however, I would not like to be defined *solely* as a parent.

The Christian tradition, for example, understands there to be a normative form of human being. It is to the doctrine of creation that theology has tended to look for its understanding of human being as a creature of God, whose very existence is derived from God and whose nature and mode of being issues from the divine intention to create a being of a certain kind. Thus, the twin doctrines of the fall and atonement speak of deviation from and restoration to this normative mode of human being. Other less absolutist ideologies are inclined to understand human being as defying any single normative definition, preferring to speak in terms of individual human differences. However – despite post-modern questioning of the possibility of the idea of 'essential human nature' – Christian theologians, on the whole, want to remain within this context. This would seem to be inevitable in the light of Christian theology's concern to present a normative picture, an 'ideal' human nature based on creation and/or salvation.

It seems to me that it is possible to group understandings of human being into four categories:

1. Subjects
2. Agents
3. Contingent
4. Social or relational

There are, of course, other ways of grouping these understandings, all with their own merits, however these categorisations work for me and so I present them to you for your consideration. It is important to note here that these are by no means mutually exclusive categories; clearly there is considerable overlap between them. What I aim to do here is to provide a framework, albeit a necessarily artificial one, that will allow us to consider the variety of ways in which human being might be understood and to point out how the genre of science fiction has involved itself in the debates.

Human being as subject: *I think, therefore I am*

The notion of human being as 'Subject' is, in many respects, an Enlightenment or modernist perspective. By this I mean it reflects the work conducted during the seventeenth and eighteenth centuries by philosophers such as René Descartes, John Locke and Immanuel Kant. It is a view which prioritises the human ego, the thinking, conscious 'I' as that which is essentially human.

It is of course true to say that in one form or another the idea of an innate 'essence' of humanness has persisted throughout human history. Sometimes it is understood in terms of the soul or spirit, at other times more specific human capacities such as rationality or creativity are singled out. Some speak of the divine spark or perhaps even conscience or a moral sense as representing the core of our humanness. Christianity has often spoken in terms of the *imago dei*, the divine image in which humanity is created and which defines what it means to be human, although what this image actually amounts to has been open to considerable debate. However, it was during the period of the Enlightenment that the dominance of the individual subject became apparent and it is to the philosopher René Descartes we must turn if we wish to understand this 'turn to the subject'.

Descartes was principally concerned with the combating of scepticism and the establishing of clear and certain knowledge, and in this respect he should properly be understood as contributing to epistemological debates. Nevertheless, it seems to me that his work has in fact wider implications for the debate concerning human nature, and this in two areas. The first relates to the question of essence: in other words, what is the most basic definition of a human being? The second relates to how we are constituted, that is to say what our component parts are. The first question is dealt with by Descartes' theory of knowledge; the second is addressed through his discussion of mind/body dualism.

In his quest for clear and certain knowledge Descartes begins by doubting all that he could not be absolutely certain of. Given that one's senses can be fooled, that all we see *could* be an illusion and that it is possible that an evil supernatural entity could be interfering with our thought processes, it would seem that everything is ambiguous and nothing can be known for certain. However, it is only when all these uncertain sources of knowledge are stripped away that Descartes believes himself to have found the one certain truth that might stand as the foundation of a new system of philosophy.

So, because our senses sometimes play us false, I decided to suppose that there was nothing at all which was such as they cause us to imagine it; and because there are men who make mistakes in reasoning . . . I rejected as being false all the reasonings I had hitherto accepted as proofs. And finally, considering that all the same thoughts that we have when we are awake can also come to us when we are asleep . . . I resolved to pretend that nothing which had ever entered my mind was any more true than the illusions of my dreams. But immediately afterwards I became aware that, while I decided thus to think that everything was false, it followed necessarily that I who thought thus must be something; and observing that this: I think, therefore I am, was so certain and so evident that all the most extravagant suppositions of the sceptics were not capable of shaking it, I judged that I could accept it without scruple as the first principle of the philosophy I was seeking.[3]

Descartes further sought to clarify the nature of human rational consciousness by differentiating between mind and body. Though he strenuously sought to avoid sounding as if he were speaking of an essential human mind or spirit somehow inhabiting a physical body, it is difficult not to view Descartes' account of the mind/body dualism in this way. If mind and body are two essentially different things how do they interact with each other in the lives of individual human beings?

Then, examining attentively what I was, and seeing that I could pretend that I had no body and that there was no world or place that I was in, but that I could not, for all that, pretend that I did not exist, and that, on the contrary, from the very fact that I thought of doubting the truth of other things, it follows very evidently and very certainly that I existed; while, on the other hand, if I had only ceased to think, although all the rest of what I had ever imagined had been true, I would have had no reason to believe that I existed; I thereby concluded that I was a substance, of which the whole essence or nature consists in thinking, and which, in order to exist, needs no place and depends on no material thing; so that this 'I', that is to say, the mind, by which I am what I am, is entirely distinct from the body, and even that it is easier to know than the body, and moreover, that even if the body were not, it would not cease to be all that it is.[4]

Without, I believe, intending to, Descartes initiated a perspective on human nature that has dominated Western thought and culture to this day. The view that a human being is, in essence, an individual rational consciousness occupying a physical shell is widespread and can be traced back, certainly in its modern form, to Descartes' work in epistemology.

As we have already mentioned, Christianity, along with many other religions, maintains an essentialist perspective on human being. God is said to have created a particular kind of being, in his/her image. Sin is seen as a deviation from this and redemption is seen as restoration to it. However, what it is that actually constitutes this essence remains at issue.

While the Enlightenment sought to identify the essence of humanness in terms of mind or Descartes' rational consciousness, what Christianity understands as the human soul seems to want to go beyond this. Contained within the notion of the human soul is the idea of unique character and identity, the breath of God which is the source of life and which survives physical death. It is not simply cognitive ability. Of course it is at this point that we may note that Christianity is itself prone to the sort of mind/body dualism we find in Descartes, although here it is of an earlier, Platonic variety.

SF often explores the question of what constitutes the human essence by manipulating factors within the human equation which have been considered essential: mind, body or memory, for example. Indeed, the mind/body dualism of Descartes is often in evidence within the genre.

Consider for a moment the long-running – although, sadly, now cancelled – BBC series *Dr Who*, first shown in 1963. When William Hartnell, the first actor to take the role of the doctor, retired, the series writer had to come up with an explanation as to why the next time we encountered the doctor he looked like Patrick Troughton, the next actor to adopt the role. Rather than simply replace the actors and hope the viewers did not notice, the writer hit on the idea of the doctor 'regenerating' at the point of death and taking on a new physical form and, to a certain extent, a new personality. What is significant here is that, arguments among fans as to who was the better doctor aside, nobody really questioned this literary device. The idea that there could be an essential personhood and more that this personhood could be transferred somehow into another 'host' body was accepted as a perfectly reasonable explanation for how the doctor could change his appearance but remain, in every important respect, the doctor. An index of how successful this device has been is witnessed to by the fact that there have been eight regenerations of the doctor (excluding Peter Cushing's portrayal in the first two films), all of whom carry the memory and experiences of their predecessors. It is quite enlightening listening to interviews with the various actors who have played the part of the doctor to hear how each of them has tried to portray continuity of identity with those who have gone before. Invariably some combination of shared memory and character traits are invoked as a signal that the doctor's essential personhood has been preserved, albeit in a new body.

Memory, it seems, plays an important part in any definition of human identity. It could be said that our identity is nothing more than the combination of our memories and experiences – or, to put it another way, are we not, to a large extent, defined by our history? Dealing with past memories has long been recognised as important to our mental health and the various counselling and psychoanalytic professions have sought to develop techniques that might better enable us to come to terms with our memories. Racial and gender identities are often constituted by a shared history, which is particularly apparent in instances of oppression where the experience of oppression has contributed significantly to a shared sense of identity. Consider, for example, the enslavement of black Africans, the holocaust and the marginalisation of women in Western culture. It would be difficult, if not impossible, to define black, Jewish or feminine identity without reference to these past histories.

In the light of all that we have said above, it is interesting to consider what might be the essential ingredients in the cooking-up of a human being. Actually I always find it easier, for some reason, to ask this question in a more negative way: what can we afford to lose and still remain human? Indeed, is it actually possible to lose one's humanity? These are fascinating and incredibly dangerous questions to ask and yet ask them we must – we have no choice. Kant tells us that we are tragically drawn to the unanswerable questions. I am not so sure that it is tragic – perhaps it is the confronting of the questions concerning our humanity that helps to define us rather than any particular answer.

Human being as agent: *I do, therefore I am*

Human being as 'agent' is, in a way, the obverse of the essentialist view. This is a characteristically existential perspective espoused particularly by Jean-Paul Sartre (1905–80) who, in a play about Descartes, stated 'Opto, ergo sum' – 'I choose, therefore I am'. This is a view which denies that human being is a fixed innate quality. In a sense we are not 'beings', we are 'becomings'. The rallying cry of existentialism has been 'Existence precedes essence': it is the making of choices that is significant.

Clearly the Christian tradition speaks of the formative nature of human activity. The things we do affect our lives and help to form who we are. Pannenberg and Moltmann both take this view of human being as in process. We are what we will become. Christianity certainly seems to me to support this eschatological perspective.

Pannenberg, in particular, clearly identifies the *imago dei* as human destiny. He says we have now moved beyond mythological ways of thinking which want to look to the past – to the beginning – to understand what we should be. What makes us human is not our past or our origins, it is our destiny and that destiny is to be in communion with God. This echoes and develops the ideas of Karl Rahner, who talked about the essence of humanity as our potential for relationship with God. This potential keeps us open to the future so that being human is being part of a 'historically becoming' process. Some theologians have picked up the language of Genesis about the 'image' and 'likeness' of God and have suggested that being in the 'image' of God refers to our potential, our destiny. The 'likeness' is the fulfilment of that potential which we are moving towards.

This is clearly one of the reasons why SF is so interesting and popular – it seeks to look forward to a point when we have moved further along the road of becoming. As we shall see in the following chapter, SF is polarised in its views of the future. We are destined either for a utopian existence, where all the ills that have beset us thus far have been dealt with, and where our mastery of technology grants us almost godlike power over reality – a view typified by Gene Roddenberry's *Star Trek* universe – or for a dystopian future, where all the ills that have beset us so far are magnified and where our mastery of technology grants almost demonic power over reality – a view typified by the cyberpunk sub-genre.

During the 1950s and 1960s, at the height of the Cold War, a great deal of apocalyptic science fiction was produced. This was the beginning of the nuclear age, when the destructive capacity of human technology, recently witnessed at Hiroshima and Nagasaki – juxtaposed with the hope that such power would put us amongst the gods – brought to full focus the ambivalence towards natural science first suggested in Mary Shelley's *Frankenstein*.

Commenting on the genre's short-story magazine *Astounding*, Brian Aldiss observes the overwhelming bleakness of its content in the light of the atomic age:

Its writers and readers ... were digesting the implications behind the nuclear bomb, its unlimited power for greatness or destruction. It was a painful process: the old power fantasies were rising to the surface of reality. Many stories were of Earth destroyed, culture doomed, humanity dying, and of the horrific effects of radiation, which brought mutation or insidious death. Nor were things depicted as much cheerier beyond the solar system.[5]

One of the images that best represents this future fear can be found in the closing scene of the film *Planet of The Apes* (1968). Having crash-landed upon what he takes to be another world, dominated by apes, the human hero, Taylor, finally discovers the truth that he has not travelled through space but through time, and the planet he is now on is, in fact, a post-apocalyptic earth. The image of Taylor confronting the ruins of the Statue of Liberty and breaking down in despair at the realisation that humanity had finally destroyed itself has become an enduring, almost clichéd symbol within SF of the human potential for self-destruction.

It has been said that writers of SF do not so much try to predict the future as prevent it from happening. Clearly much of the SF that deals with the future takes the form of a cautionary tale, a warning that if we continue as we are then this is the future that awaits us. Fritz Lang's 1926 film *Metropolis*, Aldous Huxley's *Brave New World*, published in 1932, and George Orwell's *Nineteen Eighty-Four*, published in 1948, all warn of the dangers of totalitarianism and the curtailing of personal liberty. In each of these works the loss of the right to choose is regarded as detrimental to human nature and identity.

Of course it is not only socio-political forces that might cause us to fear for our freedom to choose. With our increasing ability to manipulate human genetic material, the possibility of creating a class of human beings with a predisposition towards manual labour or even violence, for example, begins to sound less like science fiction and more like *Scientific American*. In *Brave New World* Huxley introduced us to the idea of a specially bred caste system, with Alphas representing the elite and Epsilons representing the menials. As we move into the twenty-first century SF exhibits increasing anxiety over genetic and cybernetic manipulation of human beings. While not dealing with the genetic alteration of human beings as such, Ridley Scott's classic SF film *Blade Runner* presents us with a society that creates artificial biological life forms known as 'replicants' to function as an under-class. Replicants fight humanity's wars and undertake all of its dangerous and onerous tasks. In the Film *Robocop* the critically wounded police officer Murphy is transformed into a law-enforcement cyborg complete with programmable ethical directives: 1. Serve the public trust, 2. Protect the innocent, 3. Uphold the law.

There is something deeply disturbing about the loss of self-determination, no matter to what purpose. The capacity to make choices does indeed seem to be part of humanity. Indeed, existentialist thinkers such as Martin Heidegger have argued that 'apathy', the tendency simply to go with the flow without taking responsibility for one's own existence, is to live inauthentically, to abnegate one's humanity.

In the *Star Trek: The Next Generation* episode entitled 'The Masterpiece Society' the crew of the *Enterprise* encounter a colony of genetically engineered humans. Each member of the community has been designed to be a perfect component within that community. So, the scientists, administrators and artists have known from their earliest years what they are destined to be and, moreover, are perfectly happy being what they are, because this is what they have been designed to be. The leader of the community explains that within this society no one is ever in any doubt as to their role, there are no gifted poets stuck in menial jobs, no great scientists left undiscovered, no one is in the wrong place or lives an unfulfilled life. Yet even in the face of this apparent utopia it is impossible to ignore the dehumanising potential of lack of choice. It is Captain Picard who voices these fears for us: is it not choice, the capacity to learn from our mistakes, the mystery and excitement of defining ourselves that, at least in part, makes us human? Perhaps it is the process of 'becoming' human which ultimately defines us and which is compromised whenever our self-determination is negated? This is certainly a point of view advanced by philosophers of religion such as John Hick, with his notion of a 'soul-making theodicy'[6], and to a lesser extent, with more of a focus on natural evil, Richard Swinburne. Alternatively, in making such a claim are we not simply making a virtue out of a necessity, even redefining evil as good? It is all well and good to argue that suffering and pain are character-building and that we learn by our mistakes but would we not in truth prefer to learn our lessons without discomfort, become who we want to be without struggle? As this will never be the case it is an impossible question to answer, nevertheless it does seem to me to be important that we take care in the attribution of value to pain and suffering – particularly when it is the pain and suffering of others.

In many respects every time-travel story speaks to our anxiety over the future, the intractability of the past and our struggle to master the present. Once we are aware of the process of our own becoming we can look back in anguish over missed opportunities or the wrong path taken, and look forward in anticipation or dread to the future consequences of our present actions. In H. G. Wells' novel *The Time Machine*, published in 1895, the time traveller witnesses the far future where human development has gone in two equally unpleasant directions. One group, the Eloi, live above ground and have become apathetic indolent cattle, while the other, the Morlocks, have become cannibalistic cave-dwellers, utilising the remnants of a previous civilization's technology, and feeding off the Eloi. This story echoes Wells' own fear of a popular uprising amongst the masses against the upper classes, the monstrous machine-users literally swallowing up an élite grown complacent with privilege.

It seems to me that in these time-travel stories, accessing the past has a more potent significance for our sense of self than projections of the future. Re-examining the past – and indeed revising it – can give us a sense of power over our present identity. Who can honestly say that they would not jump at the chance to return to a point in their past and alter their own personal history? We are deeply aware of the way in which our past actions make us who we are: by changing the past we change ourselves. In David Gerrold's novel *The Man Who Folded Himself*, published in 1973, this idea is taxed to its limits when the central character travels backwards and forwards in time, revising his personal history and meeting up with multiple versions of himself which represent the various alterations made to timelines:

I am Dan. And I am Don.
And sometimes I am Dean, and Dino, and Dion, and Dana.
And more . . .
There is a poker game going on in my apartment. It starts on
June 24, 1975. I don't know when it ends. Every time one of

me gets tired, there's another one showing up to take his place.
The game is a twenty-four hour marathon. I know it lasts at
least a week; on July 2, I peeked in and saw several versions of
*myself – some in their mid-twenties – still grimly playing.*⁷

Although not actually a piece of SF, a film which rather nicely
captures the significance of personal history for human
identity is Frank Capra's *It's a Wonderful Life* (referred to on
page 24). Having spent much of his life considering the needs
of others before his own, George Bailey, in a fit of despair,
decides to take his own life. By means of divine intervention
George is given a glimpse of what the world would be like had
he never been born. This revelation allows both George and
the audience to appreciate the variety of ways in which even
the most seemingly inconsequential actions shape both our
own lives and those around us. This is a motif that is revisited
in the episode *Tapestry* from *Star Trek: The Next Generation*,
where Captain Picard discovers that altering those events in
his past that he is now ashamed of as an adult serves only to
compromise the person he now is, the very person who can
look back and make such a judgement upon past events.

Films such as *The Terminator* and *Twelve Monkeys* and
television series such as *Quantum Leap* that deal with time-
travel are both taunting and compelling in their capacity to
reveal both the extent to which the past defines us and the
power that we have to take defining control over our lives
through our actions.

Human being as contingent

Human being as contingent is the characteristic behaviourist
perspective. This view understands human being as bio-
chemical organisms dependent upon context and environment
for their being. B. F. Skinner is the person normally associated
with this view. In his book *Beyond Freedom and Dignity*
(1972) as well as his SF story *Walden 2* (1948) he argues that
humans are simply animals who are determined by their con-

ditioning. Alter the environment and you produce a different kind of human being. Previously Pavlov had shown how animals could be conditioned by their environment to respond to certain stimuli – if a bell were rung every time a dog was given food, Pavlov found that after a while, simply ringing the bell would be enough to make the dog drool. That human beings are susceptible to conditioned responses is something of a commonplace observation. The practice of punishing wrongdoing and rewarding virtue and success bears witness to this fact.

The Enlightenment and its children – Marxism, for example – did much to encourage this view. There is clearly something in this. People are affected, altered, formed by their contexts. Up-bringing, education, experience all contribute to what and who we are. The Christian tradition once again seems prepared to support this notion. The conflict between Augustine and Pelagius was largely over this matter, with Pelagius arguing that it is our existence within a fallen context that makes us sinful, rather than any innate or transmitted original sin. The biblical material often speaks of people being affected by their environment. Throughout the Bible the people of God are constantly being told to set themselves apart as a holy people, to establish sacred communities and to 'be in the world but not of it'. Indeed, Christianity has always maintained that human being is a dependent being, a being that cannot sustain itself but one that is reliant upon God. The nineteenth century theologian Friedrich Schleiermacher makes this point very strongly when he speaks of the common human religious experience as being 'a feeling of absolute dependence'.[8] Human dependency is clearly a function of our creatureliness. As creatures we are intimately related to our creator and the rest of creation.

SF is fascinated by environmental effects upon human existence and the significance of place and context. Part of the attraction of the genre, it seems to me, lies in the freedom it gives to place human beings in a variety of environments and to experiment with the possible outcomes. In our imaginations we can place ourselves 'where no one has gone before'.

One of the best-known instances in which context begins to define identity is within Ray Bradbury's *Martian Chronicles* written during the early 1950s. In this sequence of stories the human beings who colonise Mars eventually begin to regard themselves as Martians, while the original indigenous Martians are constantly, and rather tragically, transformed by the increasingly human context of Mars.

It was in the early 1960s, with Frank Herbert's *Dune*, and its sequels, that issues relating to human identity and context were to receive their classic treatment within the genre. In this epic science fiction story the planet Arrakis exerts an overwhelming influence not only upon the psyche and physicality of the indigenous population but even more so upon alien colonisers. To live on Arrakis is to become part of Arrakis.

Robert Holdstock has explored similar themes in his novel *Earthwind*, published in 1977, and the whole cyberpunk subgenre of the 1990s, fronted by writers such as William Gibson, Bruce Sterling and Ruddy Rucker, gives considerable attention to the humanity/environment interface. Indeed, the preoccupation of many modern science fiction writers with virtual reality and its variants can be seen as an aspect of a larger concern with human transformation stimulated by contextual variation.

Human being as relational

Seeing human being as relational being means seeing human being as something that happens *between* rather than *in* or *to* individuals. This view has become something of a postmodern motif, with thinkers such as Emmanuel Levinas emphasising the significance of the 'other' for our own self-identity.

Clearly we are constituted by our relationships with others: parents, friends, context, enemies even. Contemporary theology and philosophy have been rather enamoured of this perspective. The Jewish philosopher/theologian Martin Buber spoke of the distinction between I-Thou and I-It encounters, where the former represents the proper mode of engagement between persons, while the latter represents the objectification of things in the world. Buber argues that we often wrongly seek to establish I-It relationships with other people, casting them in the role of things to be used and dominated. Karl Barth, drawing on the work of Buber, defines what he calls 'the basic form of humanity' as 'being in encounter'.[9] By this Barth has in mind the essential relatedness of human existence as being with God, that is to say human being is always – like it or not, know it or not – in relationship with its creator. This essential relationality also manifests itself in humanity's relationship with itself; for Barth an isolated human being is in a very real sense not human at all:

If we see man in and for himself, and therefore without his
fellows, we do not see him at all. If we see him in opposition
or even neutrality towards his fellows, we do not see him at all.
If we think that his humanity is only subsequently and
secondarily determined, as an incidental enrichment, by the
fact that he is not alone, we do not see him at all. If we do not
realize and take into account from the very outset, from the
first glance and word, the fact that he has a neighbour, we do
not see him at all.[10]

The theologian Wolfhart Pannenberg speaks of human being as destined for unity with both itself and with God. He argues that it is part of the human condition to be open to that which is beyond us – something that he refers to as 'exocentricity' as opposed to 'egocentricity', which is the tendency towards isolation and self-centredness. Exocentricity speaks of humanity in process moving towards a destiny to be truly human, truly in the divine image. This process involves an opening of the self to others, to the world around us, to the future and ultimately to God. Egocentricity, on the other hand, is nothing less than sin, a denial of our true humanity, a closedness to the future and a rejection of God:

The image of the individual who takes himself or herself to be the centre of his or her life aptly describes the structure of sin . . . In the Christian tradition this radical individualism is considered as alienation from the authentic destiny of man. When the highest value is no longer universal reason, but individual decision, radical autonomy has been often considered the peak of existential freedom. In a Christian perspective, it can be the darkest alienation from authentic existence, from one's own destiny and identity.[11]

The philosopher Emmanuel Levinas has gone even further by arguing that the other is absolutely central to our self-identification. Levinas maintains that the other, rather than being someone whom I assimilate or dominate, must be understood as having priority over me, as confronting me with absolute ethical demand, which is constitutive of my very selfhood. In a very real sense Levinas is saying that without the relational dynamic that prioritises the other over the self there is no self.[12]

This view is in radical opposition to the egotistic essentialism of the Enlightenment, which sees individual consciousness – the 'I' of Descartes' 'I think' – as the ultimate definition of human being. Clearly this view would be in keeping with the Christian tradition which sees the triune God, in whose image we are supposed to be, as a corporate being. Also the ethical nature of Christianity tends to place considerable emphasis upon relationships with God and neighbour as constitutive of human being. It can also be argued that theologically, the first thing that can be said of human being is that we are in relation with the creator.

Much of the Christian tradition's talk of sin seems to revolve around the notion of broken relationships with God and others. The German Protestant theologian Wolfhart Pannenberg speaks about sin in terms of *egocentricity* – that is to say a focusing inward upon the self rather than outward towards others, the future and ultimately God. Indeed, might not what we refer to as monstrous or inhuman be understood best in relational terms? For example, what is it that makes the Frankenstein creature seem monstrous? Its appearance? The fact of its unnatural birth? Or is it its dysfunctional relationship with its creator which is then reflected in its dealings with others? Consider what the creature has to say on encountering its estranged creator:

I am thy creature, and I will be even mild and docile to my natural lord and king, if thou wilt also perform thy part, the which thou owest me. Oh, Frankenstein, be not equitable to every other, and trample upon me alone, to whom thy justice, and even thy clemency and affection, is most due. Remember, that I am thy creature; I ought to be thy Adam; but I am rather the fallen angel, whom thou drivest from joy for no misdeed . . . I was benevolent and good; misery made me a fiend. Make me happy, and I shall again be virtuous.[13]

SF constantly explores the issue of our relationships with others/aliens and with the environment. Of course the danger of over-emphasising relationality – loss of distinct identity – is also depicted in the uniformity and totalitarianism of the Daleks and the Cybermen from *Dr Who* and the Borg from *Star Trek*, for example.

What we are and our ability to address the question is, in my view, a subject common to theology, philosophy and SF. One of the most compelling reasons for a theological consideration of SF is that SF concerns itself with issues that lie at the very heart of the theological enterprise, questions concerning the identity, origin and destiny of the human species. It is this broad arena of the human condition in general which forms the common ground between theology and SF. An engagement between theology and future fiction is, I feel, particularly significant in the raising of questions, questions which are of fundamental significance for the theologian but which perhaps may benefit from being raised from a different, unusual and imaginative perspective. Jurgen Moltmann puts it like this:

Theology always includes the imagination, fantasy for God and his kingdom. If we were to ban the images of the imagination from theology, we should be robbing it of its best possession. Eschatologically orientated theology is dependent on a messianic imagination of the future, and sets the imagination free.[14]

3
Aliens We

Others

To be 'alien' is to be 'other' than someone or something else. It does not necessarily entail being green, having tentacles for limbs or coming from another planet – although these would certainly count! Being different is something we all have to deal with, nobody else can ever be 'me'. Memories, cultural context, gender and genetic make-up all conspire to make 'me' different from 'you', 'other' than you and thus 'alien' to you.

The philosopher Hegel, for example, spoke at great length about alienation as central to his understanding of reality being in process. This process he called the dialectic, where one person or thing encounters its opposite, something alien to it, and out of this encounter is formed a third, superior synthetic someone or something from which the process begins again. Indeed Hegel makes it clear that it is only in this encounter with the other that true self-identity may be achieved. It is interesting to note that those who have attempted to build on Hegel's work, in a variety of different ways, – Feuerbach and Marx come immediately to mind – see the overcoming of alienation as central to an authentic sense of self identity. Furthermore, the significance of otherness and difference has come to occupy the forefront of continental thought in, for example, the works of Jacques Derrida and Emmanuel Levinas for philosophy and Karl Barth, Wolfhart Pannenberg and Jurgen Moltmann for theology. However, we are ahead of ourselves here.

So, what then should we make of the idea of the alien? Clearly aliens have played a central role in the genre of science fiction; indeed this has become, for good or ill, one of its defining motifs. Aliens have visited earth for a variety of reasons and human beings have visited alien worlds also for a variety of reasons. Aliens have terrorised and invaded, as well as having been on the receiving end of humanity's colonisation of the stars. In the Dr Who story *The Invisible Enemy*, the doctor explains to his companion that while he has a soft spot for human beings, *'when they gather in great numbers other species tend to get hurt.'*[1]

This sentiment, and indeed the entire story, is witness to the overwhelming significance of Darwinian evolutionary theory for the development of the genre's fascination with alien species. The doctrine of the survival of the fittest is fundamentally enshrined in the prototype of all alien invasion stories, H. G. Wells' *War of the Worlds* – due in no small part to the influence of T. H. Huxley on the young Wells. Furthermore, the portrayal of alien civilisations as hive-like collectives lacking individual identity and thus self-determination, another popular motif within the genre, can be traced back to Wells again, in his ant-like inhabitants of the Moon, the Selenites, in *First Men in the Moon* published in 1901.

It could be said that every generation creates its aliens out of the hopes and fears of its not-too-distant past. In denying his creature a mate, Frankenstein exhibits a fear that has echoed throughout SF ever since, the fear that we might be replaced, destroyed or dominated by alien competitors in the Darwinian life-or-death struggle. Many of the stories about aliens of the first half of this century fall prey to this fear: Wells' Martians; the shape-changing alien in J. W. Campbell's *Who Goes There?* (1938) – filmed as *The Thing from Another World* in 1951 and again in 1982 as *The Thing*; A. E. van Vogt's *Black Destroyer* (1939) – arguably one of the main influences on the landmark 1979 film *Alien*; Fredric Brown's *Arena* (1944) and Robert Heinlein's *Puppet Masters* (1951). All these stories, and many others produced in the popular 'pulp' magazines of the 1930s and early 1940s, bear witness to a deep-seated fear of 'the other', whether it is another race, class, ideology or gender.

Two world wars and the beginnings of the cold war did little to allay suspicions that those who were unlike us were plotting our downfall. However, whilst this theme is still to be found within the genre, the second half of the twentieth century has often seen human beings and aliens setting aside their differences in recognition of, or at least in search of, the cosmic village. Good examples of this burgeoning change of heart can be seen in A. E. van Vogt's *Co-operate or Else!* (1942), where a human and an alien find that their survival on an inhospitable world requires them to suppress their xenophobic tendencies and work together. This scenario was revisited in 1979 by Barry Longyear's *Enemy Mine*, which was subsequently made into the 1985 film of the same name. Robert Sheckley's short story *Specialist* (1953) tells of a space vessel that requires a variety of different species in order for it to function properly; human beings are known as 'pushers' because it is their unique ability that provides the propulsion for the craft.

Concerns over nuclear weapons, overcrowding and various ecological crises prompted many SF writers to portray aliens in contrast to humanity, as a means of highlighting our weaknesses and excesses, as in Olaf Stapledon's *The Flame* (1947) . In some cases, such as A. E. van Vogt's *Slan* (1940) the film *The Day the Earth Stood Still* (1951), Arthur C. Clarke's short story 'The Sentinel of Eternity', published in the same year, Robert Heinlein's *Stranger in a Strange Land* (1961) and Frank Herbert's epic *Dune* (1965), aliens – those that are other or different – are presented in a messianic mode as potential saviours of humanity. It is interesting to note that Clarke's story became the basis for the film *2001: A Space Odyssey* (1968), which is certainly one of the most significant pieces of science fiction film ever made.

The film industry was quick to pick up on the desire to see aliens as benevolent and even innocently vulnerable and this resulted in films such as *Close Encounters of the Third Kind* (1977) and *ET* (1982), both of these directed by Steven Spielberg, *The Brother from Another Planet* and *Starman* (both

1984) and Cocoon (1985). Both of the Spielberg movies have
strong religious overtones: *Close Encounters* has a theme of a
transcendental experience shared by a few culminating in
a final beatific vision where the alien visitors reveal themselves on a mountain top; *ET* has a death, resurrection and
ascension motif.

Of course, alien beings need not necessarily represent something obviously distinct from ourselves, rather they may
reflect back at us aspects of ourselves, things that we either
admire or perhaps even fear in our own character. The notion
of self-alienation has become common in Western understandings of human identity. Ever since the philosopher Hegel first
deployed the term to explain how reality as a whole comes to
an awareness of itself by overcoming its self-alienation, the
idea that human being is in some sense fragmented – alienated
either from its true potential or from its dark side – has become
a commonplace observation. Brian Stableford makes this point
about the genre of SF when he writes:

*Ideas derived from the scientific study of humankind are widely
– and sometimes very effectively – applied to the designing of
cultures which are by definition non-human. So, while most SF
aliens have always been surrogate humans, this has not
necessarily been just through idleness or lack of imagination
on the part of writers: there is a good deal of SF in which alien
beings are quite calculatedly and intelligently deployed as
substitutes for mankind.*[2]

Good examples of this can be found in A. E. van Vogt's *The
Monster* (1948), *The Lost Machine* by John Wyndham, as well
as his better-known *Midwich Cuckoos* (1957), Ray Bradbury's
Martian Chronicles produced during the late 1940s and early
1950s, Ursula Le Guin's *Left Hand of Darkness* (1969), Gene
Wolf's quartet *The Book of The New Sun* written in the 1980s,
and Stephen Donaldson's harrowing *Gap* series from the
1990s. Films such as the classic *Forbidden Planet* (1958),
Planet of the Apes (1968), *Predator* (1987) and *Mars Attacks*
(1997) also seem to me to fall into this category.

Dangerous others

The opening paragraph of H. G. Wells' *War of the Worlds*, published in 1898, reads like this:

No one would have believed, in the last years of the nineteenth century, that human affairs were being watched keenly and closely by intelligences greater than man's and yet as mortal as his own; that as men busied themselves about their affairs they were scrutinized and studied, perhaps almost as narrowly as a man with a microscope might scrutinize the transient creatures that swarm and multiply in a drop of water . . . Yet, across the gulf of space, minds that are to our minds as ours are to those of the beasts that perish, intellects vast and cool and unsympathetic, regarded this earth with envious eyes, and slowly, and surely drew their plans against us. And early in the twentieth century came the great disillusionment.[3]

Ever since Wells' Martians first turned their heat ray upon humanity at Horsell Common, SF writers have presented us with every kind of alien invasion in an attempt to stimulate and explore the fear of the other that seems so much a part of the human condition. Whilst Wells actually regarded some sort of world catastrophe as a necessary first step towards the establishment of a new utopian world order – in the first instance he saw the 1914–18 war in this light[4] – he makes the point that human beings are no strangers to callous acts of destruction directed towards other species and other races. In this Wells clearly has in mind the so-called 'gunboat diplomacy' practised by the British Empire upon less technologically advanced races. For 'Martians' read the 'British Army', for 'heat ray' read 'firearms'. Aboriginal peoples everywhere know just what it is like to face an invasion from beyond by technologically superior aliens.

And before we judge of them too harshly, we must remember what ruthless and utter destruction our own species has wrought, not only upon animals . . . but upon its own inferior

*races . . . Are we such apostles of mercy as to complain if the
Martians warred in the same spirit?*[5]

This is particularly relevant since only recently NATO forces
carried out air strikes against Serbia in response to President
Milosovic's inhumane treatment of the ethnic Albanians in
Kosovo. The wave upon wave of refugees abandoning their
homes in the face of rapacious and destructive powers which
they cannot possibly match has become one of the characteristic images of both our inhumanity and our impotence. It is
an image that Wells painted all too well for us a hundred years
ago and one which we, to our shame, have painted in human
blood throughout the twentieth century.

*There were sad, haggard women tramping by, well dressed, with
children that cried and stumbled, their dainty clothes
smothered in dust, their weary faces smeared with tears. With
many of these came men, sometimes helpful, sometimes
lowering and savage. Fighting side by side with them pushed
some weary street outcasts in faded black rags, wide-eyed,
loud-voiced, and foul-mouthed. There were sturdy workmen
thrusting their way along, wretched unkempt men clothed like
clerks or shopmen, struggling spasmodically, a wounded soldier
my brother noticed, men dressed in clothes of railway porters,
one wretched creature in a night-shirt with a coat thrown over
it. But, varied as its composition was, certain things all that
host had in common. There was fear and pain on their faces,
and fear behind them.*[6]

The notion of 'little green men from Mars' has become something of a cliché within SF in particular and Western culture
in general, and yet it undoubtedly speaks to some of our
deepest fears: the fear that those cleverer than us, stronger
than us, more powerful than us, younger than us or older than
us are, in some way, out to get us.[7] That there are ways of
understanding and living in the world other than our own calls
our way of life into question. Sometimes we are indeed in very
real peril from those who would do us harm either because

they want something that we have or simply because they can. As we are all too aware from our own history, there are equally times when we may victimise the other by demonising them through ideology and propaganda, casting them in the role of alien monsters to be mistrusted and destroyed. Anti-semitism, homophobia, misogyny, ethnic cleansing and xeno-phobias of every description speak of a fundamental alienation within humanity, a tendency to view the other as stranger, as enemy, as alien. Indeed, feminist theorists such as Mary Daly make the point that the demonisation of women by a patriar-chal culture, due in no small part to the influence of the Judaeo-Christian tradition, continues to inform the way in which women are perceived in the West and has yet to be adequately dealt with.[8]

During the height of the cold war a great deal of American SF cinema took the form of thinly veiled propaganda encouraging citizens to vigilance in the light of the perceived threat of communist infiltration. Although the film *Invasion of the Body Snatchers* made in 1955 is often seen as the archetypical communist paranoia movie of the period – with its theme of alien beings slowly replacing the inhabitants of a small American town – the considerably cheaper and less well-known film *Invaders from Mars*, made two years earlier, seems to me to be a better candidate for the title. The original the-atrical trailer for this movie attempts to shock us with images of traditional authority figures such as parents, police officers and military men performing alarming and 'alien' acts: the parents, notably the father, striking their children, the police chief and the military officer being involved in sabotage and other anti-social and un-American activities.

Invaders from Mars gives us a child's-eye view of a town being taken over by an alien intelligence where all those he has so far been taught to trust and respect now act in inhuman and unnatural ways. The scene where the boy tries to report his fears to the police only to have the now alien police chief call in his equally alien-controlled parents is a chilling one, and all the more now as the reality of child abuse becomes an acknowledged problem within our society. The message is simple but potent – beware of the alien in your midst, the price of freedom is eternal vigilance and, most notably, to be alien is to be unnatural. This message was to be restated in other films of the period, such as *It Came from Outer Space* (1953), the aforementioned *Invasion of the Body Snatchers* (1955) and *I Married a Monster from Outer Space* (1958). In each case the alien invader could take on human form but lacked human emotion and human passion. In most cases the aliens are little more than undifferentiated drones devoid of feeling, creatures of intellect alone. This fear of passionless uniformity and the loss of personal identity has persisted to the present day, as we shall see, and has become a central character trait of some of the genre's most memorable alien menaces.

It is interesting to note that in both *Invaders from Mars* and *Invasion of the Body Snatchers* the original endings of the films were altered to provide a more upbeat tone. Extra footage was added to *Body Snatchers* so that the last surviving human within the invaded town – rather than being ignored as he shouted out his warning to passing motorists – is picked up by the FBI who, believing his story, presumably take matters in hand. The final scene of *Invaders from Mars* has the young boy waking up in his bed to find that the entire story has been nothing more than a bad dream and yet, as he gazes out of his bedroom window he clearly sees an alien spaceship landing in the distance. This was considered rather too depressing for British audiences and so an alternative version was created, that removed the final shot through the window.

The insidious alien menace theme continued into the 1960s with the TV series *The Invaders* (1967–8). Here we are presented with a two-pronged fear – the fear of the alien and the fear of becoming alienated. The hero of the series is cursed with the knowledge of the existence of alien invaders who appear human and who disintegrate when killed, leaving no evidence. Throughout the 43 episodes of this series David

Vincent sought to fight the alien menace and convince the rest of the world of the truth of his claims.

To my surprise this formula has been resurrected almost wholesale in a series produced by Francis Ford Coppola entitled *'The First Wave'*. Once again we have the alien invaders taking on human form, disintegrating when killed and being fought by the lone vigilante. What makes this series interesting is the form that the aliens take and thus, by association, the kind of alienation that is being considered. The series exploits the commonly held belief in mind/body dualism, explored in Chapter 2, in that the alien invaders project their minds or consciousnesses to earth and once there, create cloned bodies to inhabit. These bodies in every respect conform to the standards of beauty currently aspired to within Western culture – in other words they are fashion models straight out of the pages of *Vogue*. What we have in *First Wave* is, in part, a revisiting of the hopes and fears of the *Frankenstein* story, where Victor seeks to create a perfect body to house his newly created life and yet abhors the creature that results from this fusion:

Although I possessed the capacity of bestowing animation, yet to prepare a frame for the reception of it, with all its intricacies of fibres, muscles, and veins, still remains a work of inconceivable difficulty and labour.[9]

How can I describe my emotions at this catastrophe, or how delineate the wretch whom with such infinite pains and care I had endeavoured to form? His limbs were in proportion, and I had selected his features as beautiful. Beautiful! – Great God! His yellow skin scarcely covered the work of muscles and arteries beneath; his hair was of a lustrous black, and flowing; his teeth of a pearly whiteness; but these luxuriances only formed a more horrid contrast with his watery eyes, . . . the beauty of the dream vanished, and breathless horror and disgust filled my heart.[10]

This association between the alien and the physically repellent has become common within SF; aliens are, more often than not, portrayed – particularly in film – as insectoid or reptilian or as amorphous visceral beings. H. G. Wells describes his Martians in this way:

Those who have never seen a living Martian can scarcely imagine the strange horror of their appearance. The peculiar V-shaped mouth with its pointed upper lip, the absence of brow ridges, the absence of a chin beneath the wedge-like lower lip, the incessant quivering of this mouth, the Gorgon groups of tentacles, the tumultuous breathing of the lungs in a strange atmosphere, the evident heaviness and painfulness of movement, due to the greater gravitational energy of the earth – above all, the extraordinary intensity of the immense eyes – culminated in an effect akin to nausea. There was something fungoid in the oily brown skin, something in the clumsy deliberation of their tedious movements unspeakably terrible. Even at this first encounter, this first glimpse, I was overcome with disgust and dread.[11]

Frankenstein's rejection of his creation and Wells' horror of the Martians may seem rather petty when understood in terms of simple physical difference – and yet is it not our reaction to physical difference which often serves to alienate from us other races, genders and indeed those with physical deformities and disabilities? Their intent on conquering Earth notwithstanding, Wells' Martians are deemed disgusting, at least in part, on the basis of their inability to cope with our earthly environment, while Frankenstein's creature is defined as a monster and a demon solely on the basis of his appearance and prior to his performing any action or uttering any word.[12]

We live in a society where appearance and image are everything. How we portray our ideals helps not only to define us but to establish what is other than us, that is to say, what is alien to us. The normalising of a particular shape or colour or gender or way of speaking or even way of smelling serves dangerously to marginalise the other, to alienate. In the episode of *Babylon 5* entitled 'Infection' a genetically engineered weapon is discovered on an alien world that has been dead for centuries. It is subsequently found that this creature, and others like it, were designed to defend their world from invading enemies. To this end they were programmed with an ideological definition of their race based upon notions of racial purity. However, once the enemy had been defeated, the creatures then turned on their own people, none of whom exactly matched up to their ideologically informed standards of perfection.

The others like you, they beat the invaders all right, just like they were programmed. They killed anything that was different, alien, but we're all aliens to each other, flawed, imperfect, different. Too tall, too short, too dark, too light, imperfect. They were killed and the killing went on and on and on . . . cleansing (it) from every imperfection in genetics . . .[13]

To return to *First Wave*, the aliens here are by no means physically unattractive, on the contrary they are quite beautiful; what is alien, repellent, monstrous even, are the consciousnesses housed within the physical shells. In one scene we are shown a warehouse full of beautiful, inanimate bodies, hosts for alien minds – a veritable body wardrobe. At one level we are being tantalised with one of the holy grails of our day, that of eternal youth and beauty, the hope that science and technology will find a way to bypass the ravaging effects of time upon our bodies, and yet at another we are being told to mistrust the outward appearance of beauty, to look beyond the surface. It would seem that as we become increasingly adept at the manipulation of human flesh at the cosmetic and genetic levels, the focus of concern has shifted from monstrous form to monstrous intent – a powerful motif also within Jesus' ethical teaching.[14]

It is not just our culture's preoccupation with youth and beauty that has been recast in the mode of something dangerous and alienating; SF has a unique capacity to take the idols and icons of a culture and expose their disturbing and dehumanising potential by casting them in the role of the alien. The notion of the alien in SF is a reflexive device: by encountering something that we take to be radically different from ourselves, we begin to recognise ourselves in the alien. The rapacious consumerism that so characterised the economics of the 1980s became a recurring motif within the SF of the 1990s where aliens no longer exterminate but rather assimilate.

The alien menace par excellence of the 1990s has to be *Star Trek's* 'The Borg'. Introduced into the series *Star Trek: The Next Generation* in the episode 'Q-Who?', the Borg are a cybernetic, collective life form, creatures of flesh and machine who operate as a single hive mentality. They are described as 'the ultimate user'. They consume planets, civilisations, technologies and individuals. The Borg collective consists of individual beings from countless consumed worlds who are modified to become part of the greater whole – drones, undifferentiated and with no individual personality. In the classic two-part *STNG* story 'The Best of Both Worlds', the Borg are encountered once again, only this time their intention is to travel to earth where they intend to 'assimilate' humanity. It is here that we first hear the Borg's now infamous universal greeting expressed almost in the form of some chilling credal affirmation:

Strength is irrelevant, resistance is futile, we wish to improve ourselves, we will add your biological and technological distinctiveness to our own, your culture will adapt to service ours . . . freedom is irrelevant, self-determination is irrelevant, you must comply.[15]

Compare this to the interrogation of Winston Smith by O'Brien in George Orwell's *Nineteen Eighty-Four*.

'Does Big Brother exist?'
'Of course he exists. The Party exists. Big Brother is the embodiment of the Party.'
'Does he exist in the same way as I exist?'
'You do not exist' said O'Brien.[16]

The truth of this litany is brought home when Captain Picard of the Enterprise, the virtual personification of enlightened individualism, is himself assimilated – at least temporarily – and becomes the voice of the Borg, the convert who eerily preaches the message of assimilation that all will become 'one with the Borg' to his crew and to humanity as a whole. In the 1996 big-screen movie *Star Trek: First Contact* the Borg appear once again and much is made of Picard's sense of violation at the hands of these creatures.

Loss of distinctiveness, of a sense of self, is at the heart of the Borg stories. The desire to understand ourselves as unique in some way and that our lives have meaning and significance is very much part of the human condition. No one wishes to believe that they arc worthless or that they have lived a meaningless existence. Indeed, the whole of the existentialist tradition in contemporary philosophy, running through thinkers as disparate as Søren Kierkegaard, Martin Heidegger and Jean-Paul Sartre, seeks to encourage authentic human existence by promoting individual choice and self-determination. It is precisely the abnegation of our capacity for self-determination that is identified by these thinkers as an essentially inhuman and inauthentic mode of existence.

In many ways *First Contact* recasts the Borg in a gothic mode, portraying them as soulless vampires who inject their prey with a form of techno-virus that drains them of their humanity, leaving them pallid and passionless, empty shells to be cybernetically augmented and set to work as part of the collective. It is disturbing to catch glimpses of Borg who still wear the tatters of Star Fleet uniforms, whose faces one recognises from earlier in the film as members of the crew.

In the episode 'I-Borg'[17] a Borg drone is discovered badly injured and is taken aboard the Enterprise to be treated. The Captain, in the light of his previous experiences, will have nothing to do with the creature and a plan is drawn up to return the drone to the Borg collective as a Trojan horse, modified to introduce a destructive virus that would eventually destroy the entire collective. No one, aside from the

ship's doctor, has a problem with this course of action: geno-
cide it may well be but it is argued that in war, particularly
with a superior adversary, all is fair. However, as the now
isolated Borg drone becomes increasingly individuated, is
given a name – as opposed to its functional Borg designation
'Third of Five' – makes friends and starts to refer to itself as
'I' rather than 'we', the situation changes and the plan is
abandoned.[18]

The reacquisition of identity humanises the Borg who
becomes person rather than drone, an end rather than a means
to an end.[19] It is always more difficult to deal with a person
face to face than it is to deal with them via some more anony-
mous means. Hence we make use of mediators, lawyers,
memos, notices, answer-phones, letters, e-mail, and of course
weapons such as cruise missiles, to create a buffer between us
and the face of the other so that we do not have to stare into
that face and feel the pain that we are inflicting. The Borg are
by turns the faceless demonic enemy against which all actions
are justified, the faceless bureaucracies that refuse to feel our
pain and anguish and that see all these things as irrelevant,
and the rapacious powers that are beyond conscience and morality and beyond our capacity to master. They exist merely to
continue to exist and regard all things as consumable to this
end. Perhaps all that can be done in the face of such an unstop-
pable juggernaut is to stand in its way, as Gandhi did against
the British Empire, as many did before the Nazis and as the
young man did who set himself against a tank in Tiananmen
Square.

The 1996 film *Independence Day*, while not a particularly
thoughtful piece of SF, also presents us with an alien species
intent upon consuming the Earth. The creatures are, as always,
technologically superior to ourselves and operate as a hive
having no distinct individuality. This hive species is juxtaposed with a rather gung-ho American rugged individualism
portrayed as present in a wide variety of people, from exotic
dancers to the First Lady, from drunks to the President, from
nerdy scientists to top-gun fighter pilots. Each individual is

painted larger than life, distinct, unique, while one alien
is very much like another. When the President attempts to
communicate with the aliens to find out what it is they want
humanity to do, the answer is simply 'die'.

I saw its thoughts, I saw what they're planning to do. They're
like locusts, they're moving from planet to planet, their whole
civilization. After they've consumed every natural resource they
move on.

This could so easily be a description of industrial or corporate
colonialism: the stripping of the rainforests, the pressure to
produce cash crops to service Western consumerism, the
clothing sweat-shops of India and the rest of Asia. In many
ways those of us living in the West both 'consume every
natural resource' and seek to transplant our 'whole civilisation'. There is an arrogance that accompanies the Western
mind-set which issues out of its modernist roots. Ever since
the Enlightenment elevated human reason to almost godlike
stature there has been a tendency to regard Western culture
as almost transcendental or, as post-moderns such as Jean-
François Lyotard would have it, as a grand narrative. The term
'grand narrative' refers to one way of looking at and inter-
preting the world and our place in it. Thus, Western science
and technology, Western medicine, Western tastes and standards of excellence, Western criteria for success, and indeed
the whole Western lifestyle model are regarded as in some
sense normative. Other cultures are regarded as quaint or
underdeveloped or even primitive in comparison to our own.
Western colonialism has often been spoken of as bringing 'civilisation' to these other cultures and yet what is actually meant
is that we are bringing '*our* civilisation' to these cultures.
This theme is explored strikingly in novels such as Robert
Heinlein's *Logic of Empire* (1941), Robert Silverberg's *Invaders*
from Earth (1958), Ursula Le Guin's *The Word for World is*
Forest (1972) and John Brunner's *The Shockwave Rider* (1975)
– the latter based on ideas found in Alvin Toffler's *Future*
Shock (1970).

The 1998 TV mini-series *Invasion Earth* is a rather more intelligent portrayal of alien invasion than the previously mentioned *Independence Day*. Here we have an alien race, once again hive-like and technologically advanced, surreptitiously manipulating human development so that human beings might be harvested of certain chemicals produced by their bodies – a theme revisited in the 1999 film *The Matrix*. The discovery of this covert activity by an extra-terrestrial invader prompts a sequence of military responses which do nothing other than bring the aliens and their invasion plans out into the open. A vast organic device is deployed by the invaders to literally suck the life out of Earth. Unlike *Independence Day*, in which human ingenuity and resourcefulness win the day, *Invasion Earth* leaves us with the rather bleak prospect of humanity pursuing a scorched-earth policy, detonating nuclear devices in the path of the alien invader, not to destroy it – this has proved to be impossible – but to deny it our planetary resources. As an aside it should be noted here that on the whole, British SF tends to be rather bleaker than its American counterpart. The SF writer and critic J. Gunn makes this point when he writes:

The Wells of The Time Machine, The Island of Dr. Moreau, The War of the Worlds, When the Sleeper Awakes, *and* The First Men in the Moon *gave science fiction, and British SF, what Damon Knight has called 'the mood of pessimistic irony' that much of American SF has lacked.*[20]

In 1979 Dan O'Bannon, Ridley Scott and Hans Giger gave SF probably the most memorable alien of all time. In the film entitled simply *Alien* – as well as three sequels to date – we are presented with an alien menace which taps into our most primal fears: fear of the unknown, fear of superior power, fear of exploitation and fear of violation. Drawing on earlier stories such as van Vogt's *Black Destroyer* as well as his own contribution to the 1974 spoof SF film *Dark Star*, O'Bannon has created an alien creature that is totally inimical to other forms of life. The first film of the series tells the story of the crew of the deep space vessel the *Nostromo*, returning home to earth after some undisclosed commercial mission. The ship is diverted to an unknown planet in response to a distress signal where the crew discover a nest of eggs in the body of a derelict spaceship. The product of one of these eggs is the eponymous alien which first attaches itself to a human host, then lodges itself in the host's chest, subsequently erupting from and thereby killing its host. The creature proceeds throughout the film to kill all but one member of the crew, Ellen Ripley, who goes on to become the heroine of the sequels.

The alien here is a parasite intent upon its own survival. The queen alien – revealed in the second film – produces thousands of these eggs which lie dormant, waiting for an unsuspecting host to come by. Many have seen the alien here as a metaphor for everything from cancer to rape and in truth it could be any or all of these. The key here, to my mind, is that this alien creation is able, most potently, to conjure up our deepest fears concerning otherness and powerlessness, it confronts us with all the horrors of being used as a disposable resource and in that way has become one of the most powerful and nightmarish symbols within the SF genre. This motif is driven home further when it is revealed that the very company that Ripley and the rest of the crew work for – a company with substantial government defence contracts – is responsible for their being diverted from their homeward journey in the first place. The company – as becomes clearer in the second film, *Aliens* – wishes to capture and breed the aliens for use as weapons. Thus we find it is not just the alien being that indiscriminately uses human beings for its own ends but other human beings as well: humanity becomes alienated from itself.[21]

Defining humanity and inhumanity

The fear of being used or exploited by another merely as a resource affects us at many levels. Sexual, economic and emotional exploitation of individuals, ethnic groups and genders has led to some of the worst atrocities in human history and has prompted many thinkers to attempt to define the essence of humanity so that its opposite, inhumanity, might also be identified.

The philosopher Immanuel Kant, one of the central figures of the Enlightenment, contributed a great deal to our understanding of human persons when he argued that we ought always to treat others as 'ends-in-themselves' rather than as 'means to an end', as persons with dignity not as things to be used. It is in the nature of 'things' to be conditioned, dependent upon the laws of nature and thus to be ultimately of relative value. Rational beings, on the other hand, by virtue of their unconditioned nature, their free will, as ends and not merely means, may lay claim to the status of persons. Only rational beings, argues Kant, possessing autonomy of will such that they can act ethically, are to be regarded as ends in themselves and as beings of absolute worth.

Now I say that man, and in general every rational being, exists as an end in himself, not merely as a means for arbitrary use by this or that will: . . . Beings whose existence depends, not on our will, but on nature, have none the less, if they are non-rational beings, only a relative value as means and are consequently called things. Rational beings, on the other hand, are called persons because their nature already marks them out as ends in themselves. Persons, therefore, are not merely subjective ends whose existence as an object of our actions has a value for us: they are objective ends – that is, things whose existence is in itself an end . . .[22]

For Kant the attribution of intrinsic worth or dignity to persons, as opposed to merely an arbitrary or relative price, stems precisely from this understanding of the rational being as autonomous law-maker, and thus as an end in itself. That which has a mere price may be substituted for something of equivalent price. However, to have dignity is to be beyond all price and equivalence. Only humanity, therefore, in its unconditioned mode as law-maker and determiner of all value can have dignity: 'that is, an unconditioned and incomparable worth – for the appreciation of which, as necessarily given by a rational being, the word "reverence" is the only becoming expression.'[23]

The notion of rational beings as ends rather than means further gives rise to Kant's understanding of the society of persons as a kingdom of ends. By 'kingdom' Kant intends 'a systematic union of different rational beings under common laws'.[24] A rational being is a member of this kingdom when, as a maker of universal law, he also subjects himself to that law in its following expression: 'Act in such a way that you always treat humanity, whether in your own person or in the person of any other, never simply as a means, but always at the same time as an end.'[25] So, argues Kant, the rational being, as end in itself and consequently as person, must regard all other rational beings similarly as ends, as autonomous law-makers. We must 'reverence' each individual and ascribe to them the 'dignity' and 'worth' which is intrinsically theirs by virtue of their personhood, this personhood being constituted by their consciousness of themselves as free moral law-makers – in other words, as transcendental selves.

For Kant relationality would appear to amount then to the formal recognition of human dignity; that is to say, of the other as being of intrinsic worth. We must hold in the highest esteem, we must 'reverence' the other, who, as a rational being, must be acknowledged as possessing the same autonomy of the will and therefore as being part of the same intelligible world as that which we are conscious ourselves of occupying.

Within the Judaeo-Christian tradition the notion of human beings as having been created in the divine image has been deployed in an attempt to attribute unique value and status to individual human existence. Christian theological anthropology is strongly rooted in a notion of normativeness; in other words, it understands there to be a normative form of human being. In the main it is to the doctrine of creation that Christian theology has looked for its understanding of human being as a creature of God, whose very existence depends upon God and whose nature and existence are the results of the divine intention to create a being of a particular kind. So, the doctrines of the fall and the atonement speak of deviation from and restoration to this normative mode of human being. As I have argued elsewhere, the very make-up of the Christian story – creation, fall and redemption – demands the use of normative language and is at the very heart of Christianity's ability to function ethically and politically.[26]

We are not alone

We are told in the opening chapters of Genesis that the first thing God identified as 'not good' about creation was that human beings were alone. Loneliness and isolation eat away at the very fabric of our sense of self. With no one to communicate with, to react to and to sympathise with, our unique sense of personal identity loses focus. Isolation has long been recognised as an essential part of the torturer's tool kit, where solitary confinement and other forms of sensory deprivation are deployed as a means of breaking the human spirit and weakening the sense of self.

Isolation is on the increase within our culture. One of the most notable features of the period since the Second World War has been the increase in the number of people living alone: in 1986 nearly a quarter of households in Great Britain contained only one person, compared with about one tenth in 1951. At the same time the proportion of households containing five or more people has halved, and is now less than one tenth.[27]

This tendency towards increasing privatisation supports the findings of J. H. Goldthorpe and D. Lockwood who, in the early 1960s, began their now famous study of the 'affluent manual worker'. The original point of the project was to test the validity of the 'Embourgeoisement thesis' which held that with the advent of higher wages and the accompanying improvement in the standard of living, the traditional working classes were being assimilated into a broad middle class, with respect to their ideals and social activities. The results of the study demonstrated, however, that while this was not in fact the case, with the working class maintaining its own distinct set of values, it was found that with an increase in material prosperity the working classes did exhibit a strong tendency towards increased privatisation.

It would be difficult to sustain the idea that the affluent workers we studied typically possessed dual social identity – still working class in their role as rank-and-file production employees but in their out-of-work roles indistinguishably part of the middle-class society . . . Rather than such an assimilation, our findings would indicate as the most probable concomitant of these workers' orientation to work and of their present type of employment what we have earlier referred to as privatisation – a process, that is, manifested in a pattern of social life which is centred on, and indeed largely restricted to, the home and the conjugal family.[28]

Privacy is no longer the accepted right of a privileged few, everyone's home is now their castle. With the concept of privacy being pushed back within the borders of individual self-consciousness, partly as a result of the Cartesian *cogito*, as we saw in the previous chapter, privacy and property are no longer so intimately linked. Arthur Britten points out that,

The belief in the interiorisation of a world of meaning and uniqueness of experience is embodied in the language and literature of Western society . . . Privacy is not only taken for granted, it is elevated to a moral category. The violation of an individual's privacy is viewed in the same way as the desecration of the sacred by the unfaithful.[29]

In his book *The Private Future*, Martin Pawley examines this issue further, drawing out the concomitant effect of privatisation – that being the evacuation of the public realm. 'There is now nothing but a vacant terrorized space between the government – which controls and maintains production – and the isolated consumer, who increases his consumption in proportion to his isolation.'[30] The advent of suburban man is, says Pawley, the direct result not of an eroding of so-called traditional values by the barbaric elements within society, but rather of the development of industry, consumerism and the media. The intensive utilisation of what Pawley refers to as 'energy slaves' – that is, items such as cars, washing machines and vacuum cleaners – reduces the need for social interaction and dependence.[31] Trapped on this path of isolation, Western society must consume at an ever-increasing rate to maintain the level of detachment necessary for social harmony. The breakdown of the extended family consisting not simply of husband, wife and children, but also of grandparents and even aunts and uncles, coupled with a general trend towards a lower level of occupancy, speaks of a terrible movement towards isolationism all but completed in the latter half of the twentieth century.

Today, the home is seen, for all practical purposes, as a total environment in which one's basic and recreational needs are amply provided for by the technological marvels of our age. It is now possible to live one's life in a manner considered successful and comfortable by Western standards without ever leaving the confines of the home. Computer links are available via the internet, through which one may conduct business, collaborate on a book with a colleague hundreds of miles away, pay the bills, do the shopping and send letters and documents without even having to go to a post-box. Videos and DVD make it unnecessary to visit a cinema or the theatre, hi-fi can reproduce operatic, orchestral and rock music with pinpoint clarity while one pops a pre-packed gourmet meal into the microwave oven ready for an evening of isolated entertainment.[32]

What is missing from this individualistic utopia is the transcendent other. Indeed, personal stereo allows one to remain within a cosseted individualised world even while indulging in the unsavoury business of entering the public sphere. Pawley points out that even such an innocuous invention as central heating, by heating every part of the house, makes it unnecessary for members of a family to congregate in one place. Thus the elderly are shunted off to old folks' homes and children abandon their parents' home as soon as possible in search of their own autonomy, their own total environment. Despite the rabid individualism outlined above, the notion of community is still an attractive if elusive one. However, it is now almost completely in the hands of the image-makers, the media men:

Recognition of the fact that this community ... has become an illusion, an image, a roll of tape, a spool of film, a splendid but empty palace, is too painful. Hence the retention of the language and pageantry of community and obligation to describe an increasingly gim-crack facade of public events for which self-interest is the only comprehensible motivation. This massive self-deception, the best-kept secret of our century, is only betrayed by behaviour, never by words – for 'we' intentionally lack the words to describe it. Behaviour in this sense has become increasingly divorced from the language that purports to explain it as part of the same self-protecting process. A triumph of security.[33]

Thus, while we are assured through advertisements that by using a certain brand of washing powder our family life will be enhanced, the presupposition being that this is a desirable state of affairs, in actuality we continue to seek complete irresponsibility. The most comforting phrase in our society is 'without obligation'. In this sense, the rejection of the transcendent other permits us to live our lives without the need for relating or indeed, more disturbingly, without the social and emotional apparatus to begin to relate to those beyond us.

The disintegration of our sense of community, of otherness, coupled with the atrophying of the correlative social structure, has created a poisonous no-man's-land of traditional public places. The public sphere is now a place of all-powerful and malevolent bureaucracy, escalating prices and mob violence. Comfort and security are available only within the environment that has been tailored to one's individual needs – in other words, the home – although to an equally significant degree, the car provides a similar cocoon-like environment. Pawley speaks of a 'secondary reality' that is constructed by the individual to counter the undeniable horrors of a public realm left to run wild. It is this secondary reality that is fed by the media, consumerism and of course politicians, the latter of whom have discovered that what wins elections is not issues but tax-cuts and higher wages.

The privatized individual vacates the public realm which thus falls progressively into the hands of a bureaucracy laced with speculative corruption. Such administration in turn leads to more news of families evicted and old ladies living in their bathrooms and thus confirms the wisdom of the initial withdrawal itself. Because the public realm is less and less often experienced and more and more reported it becomes an image consisting of rapes, hi-jackings, riots, speeches, murderers and rackets . . . Like unprofitable railways which can only be kept running with massive subsidies, collapsed communities are attended by increasing numbers of social workers who are paid to prop up a structure collapsing of its own weight . . . the old patterns of community care patched up repeatedly by infusions of public money and professional skill.[34]

Those who have most successfully fortified themselves against the outside world are also protected from the horrors of its disintegration by the controlled and emotionless reporting of the news on television and radio, where the announcement of thousands of deaths through flood, starvation and war is given out in the measured tones of society's professional shock absorbers.

Alien saviours

This is a very grim picture indeed and one which has been painted for us in a variety of different ways within SF – notably within the sub-genre of cyberpunk in works by William

Gibson and Bruce Sterling. Faced with the very real experience of the breakdown in human communality and the creation of a threatening no-man's land where public space used to be, the notion of the alien other as friend and saviour has become increasingly popular.

One of the most popular and enduring alien saviour figures must be 'Superman', created by Jerry Siegel and Joe Shuster and first appearing in the June 1938 edition of *Action Comics*. Superman formed the template for a veritable army of 'super-heroes' during the 1940s and 1950s, coming to a head in the work of Jack Kirby and Stan Lee who created such characters as 'The Fantastic Four' and 'The Amazing Spider-Man'. With the character of Superman we are presented with the arche-typical transcendental saviour figure. The baby Kal-El – Superman's real name – the lone survivor of the doomed world Krypton, is discovered by the childless Mr and Mrs Kent and is brought up as their own son. Owing to the unique effects of our sun on a Kryptonian body, Clark Kent, as he is now known, finds that he possesses powers and abilities that go far beyond that of ordinary human beings. Armed with these 'super powers' and driven by the ethics instilled in him by his human parents, Clark Kent clothes himself in the colours of the American flag and begins his crusade for 'Truth, Justice and the American way'.

The whole superhero tradition, starting with Superman, speaks to a basic human desire to find some power from beyond ourselves that will reach into our world and deal with the problems that beset us. Superman, and to a much greater extent the Batman, are figures of both justice and power that stand outside of the mundane world. The superhero is the ultimate *deus ex machina*, invulnerable, powerful and incor-ruptible. In a world where the rich and the powerful seem above the law and where even those who are elected or employed to protect us are themselves found to be powerless – or worse, corruptible – the dream of an ethical power which transcends this situation is a potent one.[35]

The philosopher Ludwig Feuerbach, arguably the architect

of modern atheism, argued that humanity's belief in a transcendent supreme being, a God, is in fact nothing more than a tragic exercise in self-alienation. In the wake of the advances made by the natural sciences, and with optimism in human ability riding high, a disjunction is experienced between our potential as a species and our limitations and failures as individual human beings. Thus, argued Feuerbach, we become alienated from our potential; we push it way from ourselves and call it God. The observation that human beings are dependent upon something beyond themselves has become an important theme within modern thought, either as an account of a tragic lack of maturity amongst human beings in the atheistic writings of Feuerbach, Freud and Sartre, or as a description of the essence of humanity as fundamentally relational in thinkers such as Schleiermacher, Pannenberg and Levinas. Indeed, in Emmanuel Levinas we find one of the most potent expressions of the notion that 'I' am dependent upon the 'other': 'My ethical relation of love for the other stems from the fact that the self cannot survive by itself alone, cannot find meaning within its own being-in-the-world, within the ontology of sameness.'[36] The point is that as an individual, the self-contained 'I' – Descartes' *cogito* – we lack true humanity, a humanity which is properly constituted out of the dynamic which takes place between 'I' and 'other'. Levinas goes further in arguing that this humanising engagement must take an ethical form in its prioritising of the other rather than a dominating of that other by the self. Such an encounter with the other inevitably places the self at risk but is ultimately unavoidable for the truly ethical self:

To expose myself to the vulnerability of the face [of the other] *is to put my ontological right to existence into question. In ethics, the other's right to exist has primacy over my own, a primacy epitomized in the ethical edict: you shall not kill, you shall not jeopardize the life of another . . . Ethics is, therefore,* against nature *because it forbids the murderousness of my natural will to put my own existence first.*[37]

The phrase 'we are not alone' has become something of a mantra for post-*X-Files* believers in benevolent extra-terrestrial intelligence and one which has been lampooned of late in films such as *Independence Day* and the wonderfully retro *Mars Attacks!*. In *Independence Day* a scene which calls to mind the beatific vision sequence in *Close Encounters* – one in which an alien ship hovers above a group of exceptional human beings and begins to communicate in light and sound – similarly explodes into light and sound as the aliens unleash their primary weapon, destroying people, buildings and the banners and placards of welcome. Tim Burton's *Mars Attacks!*, arguably the first really post-modern SF film, as we shall see later, treats us to a scene where the Martians are welcomed to Earth and a white dove is released as a symbol of peace. As the bird soars above the alien emissary he draws his ray gun and fries it to a crisp before he and his companions then proceed to fry everyone else.

While alien visitors have never ceased to be regarded with suspicion within the genre – even those claiming to come in peace, such as the alien Visitors in the 1985 mini-series *V* and the more recent Taelons in Gene Roddenbery's *Earth: Final Conflict*, are discovered ultimately to be using humanity – the desire for connection and even salvation from beyond this world still remains a strong one. Arthur C. Clarke's *2001: A Space Odyssey* (1968), developed from his 1951 short story 'Sentinel of Eternity' depicts a humanity that is dependent upon a mysterious, almost godlike alien intelligence for its evolutionary development. The story begins with humanity's apish ancestors encountering an alien device, a black mono-lith, which catalyses its evolution into a tool-using species. It ends with human beings encountering the monolith again in space; however, this time the transformation that it precipi-tates is to a new level of existence symbolised in the birth of a star child that appears to transcend physicality. Clarke is particularly fond of the notion of human dependency upon godlike alien beings and he explores this theme in other stories such as *Against the Fall of Night* (1948) and *Childhood's End* (1950).

In the 1951 film *The Day the Earth Stood Still*, based on Harry Bates' story *Farewell to the Master* (1940), Earth is visited by the messianic alien figure Klaatu. In a particularly powerful scene, Klaatu exits from his flying saucer, which has been ringed with military hardware and anxious onlookers, and announces that he comes in peace, upon which, probably rather rashly, he flourishes a strange device which is mistaken for a weapon, and he is immediately shot and wounded. At this point we are introduced to the menacing figure of Gort, Klaatu's robot – although the original Bates' story ends with the revelation that it is in fact the robot who is the master – who proceeds to melt the threatening guns and tanks while, for now at least, stopping short of actually killing anyone. Klaatu recovers and asks to meet with the world's leaders to present them with a message; this proves problematic as none of the individual governments trust one another and all want the meeting to take place on their own soil. Exasperated with the pettiness of Earth's leaders, Klaatu escapes from his guards and seeks to learn more of humanity by living amongst ordinary people. Ultimately Klaatu is betrayed, hunted down and eventually killed, only to be resurrected when Gort returns his body to the safety of his space vessel. Klaatu's final message to humanity contains a warning that the other planets will not tolerate Earth's warlike and destructive tendencies, especially now that they have taken their first steps into outer space. Inter-planetary peace has, apparently, been achieved through the creation of a robot police force, of which Gort is a member and these robots have absolute authority in all matters relating to inter-planetary aggression.

. . . in matters of aggression we have given them absolute power over us. This power cannot be revoked . . . The result is, we live in peace without arms or armies, secure in the knowledge that we are free from aggression and war, free to pursue more profitable enterprises. We do not pretend to have achieved

perfection but we have a system and it works. I came here to give you these facts. It is no concern of ours how you run your own planet, but if you threaten to extend your violence this earth of yours will be reduced to a burnt-out cinder.[38]

Moral absolutes and corporate morality

Putting aside, for the moment, the questionableness of (a) assigning the task of galactic law-enforcement to machines, and (b) enforcing peace with the threat of extinction, the theme of a transcendental moral absolute is a powerful one. Certainly the Judaeo-Christian tradition speaks of a higher authority in matters of ethics, violence is prohibited and, on one reading of the tradition at least, we are told that 'he who lives by the sword shall die by the sword'. Part of the attraction of a religion is that it provides a sense of the absolute, a system of beliefs which allow human beings to interpret the world as possessing order, meaning and sense – a theme we shall return to in a subsequent chapter. While we often balk at authority structures that demand a particular mode of behaviour from us, we nevertheless seem drawn to absolute codes of conduct, as is evidenced in our attitudes to world events and in our use of language. The recent war in former Yugoslavia parallels the story of Klaatu in many respects. The aggression of one people towards another prompts an ethical judgement from powerful onlookers. Just as Klaatu demonstrates his power by neutralising the world's electrical power for an hour – hospitals and planes in flight excluded – effectively bringing the planet to a standstill (hence the title of the film), so too have Nato forces sought to bring Serbia to a standstill by air strikes aimed at its military installations and infrastructures. As Klaatu threatened earth with violence if it extended its aggression beyond its borders, so too has Nato threatened Serbia with an all-out land war. What fuelled Klaatu's ultimatum to earth equally fuels Nato's stance against Serbia – a sense of moral superiority coupled with superior power.

To condemn violence, prejudice, injustice and inequality requires some sort of moral standard against which to judge these things. To speak of certain acts as inhumane or monstrous requires at least a provisional definition of human being; to convict a person of crimes against humanity implies a sense of corporate morality such that one could be called to account by the many. Ever since the Enlightenment began to question and ultimately dismiss religious authorities, the quest for ethical absolutes subsequent to the so-called 'death of God' has been an ongoing one. The philosopher Immanuel Kant (1724–1804), having established grounds for epistemological certainty in the *Critique of Pure Reason* sought in the *Critique of Practical Reason* to establish a basis for ethical certainty that was not wholly dependent upon God.

The English philosopher Jeremy Bentham (1748–1832) championed an ethical system, Utilitarianism, based upon the principle of the greatest happiness for the greatest number. The intention here is to remove ethics from the realms of vague metaphysical and religious speculation and provide it with a scientific and empirically calculable foundation. In spite of its many inherent weaknesses, the most damning of which is a tendency to marginalise the minority in favour of the majority, Utilitarianism is still called upon to do service as a pragmatic ethical tool within our culture.

It is not until we hear from Friedrich Nietzsche (1844–1900), notably in his *Thus Spake Zarathustra* (1883–91) and *Beyond Good and Evil* (1886), that we encounter a thorough-going attempt at rejecting all manner of ethical absolutes, both the religious kind, founded upon the notion of a divine law-giver, and the enlightened kind, based upon ideas of duty and consensus. Nietzsche not only rejects Christianity on the grounds of its representing a 'slave morality' typified in its central figure, the crucified Christ, he is equally dismissive of the Enlightenment's attempts at replacing a set of religious absolutes with a set of secular ones.

Nietzsche regarded Enlightenment-resourced modernism as a kind of twilight existence inhabited by a herd, slavishly following one way of knowing and behaving. This he saw as the result of almost two millennia-worth of adherence to a single religious absolute, that of Christianity. The Enlightenment's quest for ethical and epistemological absolutes is, he argues, motivated by fear – in particular, the fear of anarchy attendant on the dissolution of the absolutes that maintained Christian Europe. Robert Pippin makes this point very clearly when he gives an account of Nietzsche's understanding of modernity:

If the fundamental problem is modern 'morality', then 'Morality in Europe today is herd animal morality' . . . Since modern Christian democratic man has become so unsure of his various 'idols' (e.g. natural right, the state, humanity, science, reason), or unwilling to deal with what is emerging as the disintegration of the justification traditionally provided for such idols, he has taken refuge in another form of security, a 'last' form of justification. What he now affirms are the kinds of ideals that the maximum number of people could affirm without conflict . . . Nietzsche implies that in the anxiety created by doubts about divine authority, and in the chaos created by so many irreconcilable attempts at a secular basis of moral order, we have, in a kind of panic, taken refuge in each other, in safety, or the lowest common denominator.[39]

The ethical relativism that Nietzsche's philosophy seems to advocate as the only real alternative to one informed by religious absolutes is characteristic of the many-headed creature known as post-modernism. It is for this reason, as well as others, that Nietzsche is often regarded as one of the principle architects of the post-modern movement, a movement that has as one of its defining motifs what Jean-François Lyotard calls an 'incredulity towards metanarratives',[40] that is to say a rejection of absolutes and universals, be they ethical or epistemological.

Of course encounters with aliens, as we have pointed out at the beginning of this chapter, are precisely confrontations with alternative perspectives, differing narratives that cause us to reflect upon our own – sometimes out of fear, other times out of hope for something better – and to ask the question: 'Is this the only way?' Our response to this question and indeed the very way in which that response manifests itself determines the manner in which we engage with the world and those others that we find in it. Is the category of alien inevitably to be regarded as equivalent to monster or invader? Are we so afraid of challenge and change and so confident in what we *know* that any confrontation with the alien other that might catalyse a change is to be feared and the alien demonised? In the 1997 film *Men in Black*, K – a senior member of the eponymous organisation whose job it is to police the alien community living in secret amongst us – explains the need for secrecy to a new recruit:

'Okay kid, here's the deal. At any given time there are around 1500 aliens on the planet – most of them right here in Manhattan – and most of them are decent enough, they're just trying to make a living . . . Humans, for the most part, don't have a clue, they don't want one or need one either. They're happy, they think they have a good bead on things.'

'Why the big secret? People are smart, they can handle it.'

'A person is smart, people are dumb, panicky, dangerous animals and you know it. 1500 years ago everybody knew *that the earth was the centre of the universe. 500 years ago everybody* knew *the earth was flat and 15 minutes ago you* knew *that people were alone on this planet. Imagine what you'll* know *tomorrow.'*

The balance between maintaining some systems of absolutes while not allowing this to collapse into an inflexible totalism is not easy to achieve. Nevertheless, it seems to me that it would be a great shame indeed if K's observation quoted above were truly the case – if otherness and difference required suppression in order to preserve an unquestioned existence born out of fear and an arrogant confidence in our particular perception of reality and our place in it. I would suggest that it is to such attitudes of intolerance that we ought properly to look in search of our monsters rather than to any notion of the alien.

4
Where Are We Going and How Do We Get There?

In his journal entry for 1 August 1835, the philosopher and theologian Søren Kierkegaard had this to say:

What I really lack is to be clear in my mind what I am to do, not what I am to know, except in so far as a certain understanding must precede every action. The thing is to understand myself, to see what God really wishes me to do; the thing is to find a truth which is true for me, to find the idea for which I can live and die.[1]

Whether there is a right or ideal or most satisfying way for us to live, either as a species or as an individual member of a species, is a question that concerns humanity in a very basic way. All religions, ideologies and political and philosophical systems are intent upon providing us with possible, and more often than not competing, answers to this question. Any attempt at addressing the question of human purpose and the manner in which that purpose might best be achieved must inevitably be dependent upon preliminary questions relating both to the nature of existence as a whole and to human value and significance within it.

Order, meaning and sense

As human beings we are constantly engaged, at one level or another, with the quest for *order*, *meaning* and *sense*. We tend to seek out, and indeed seem to require, patterns and consistencies throughout our lives; we are irritated when time-tables are not adhered to, when maps and other kinds of instructions are inaccurate and when certain forms of action do not give rise to the expected outcome. Modern science and the technologies that it has produced are dependent upon an ordered notion of the cosmos, a belief that a certain cause will give rise to a predictable effect and that the order of things will remain consistent. We would find it difficult if not impossible to live in a world in which the laws that seem to govern reality were in constant flux – *Alice's Adventures in Wonderland* provide us with an insight into such a world, it seems to me.[2] What we require of reality is that it conforms consistently to a set of rules that will allow us to live coherent lives. It is for this reason that we become exasperated with people and institutions that do not behave in a consistent manner, that 'change the rules' or 'move the goalposts'. One of the highest forms of praise that we can give to a friend, or an enemy for that matter, is that 'you know where you are with them'.

In the 1999 film *The Matrix*, recognition that what is being perceived as reality is in fact a computer-generated illusion gives those with that knowledge the ability to transcend the apparent natural laws of that world. While being trained to fight those who police the virtual world of the Matrix, the hero Neo is taught to move as fast as thought because in a world that exists only in the mind physical laws – despite what one's mind might try to tell one – do not apply. In one scene Neo has a conversation with a small boy who appears to be bending a spoon by thought alone; on being asked how this is possible, the boy replies that the trick is not to try to bend the spoon but to realise that there is no spoon.

In the Hebrew Scriptures the book of Job is, at least in part, an attempt to explore the effect of an apparent breakdown in the order of things. Job, it would appear, having been a godly man, finds it impossible, as do his friends, to understand why he is apparently being punished by God – this is not how it is supposed to be. 'If I have sinned, what have I done to you, O watcher of men? Why have you made me your target? Have I become a burden to you? Why do you not pardon my offences and forgive my sins?' (Job 7:20–21). Tragically, of course, the failure to make adequate sense of bad fortune and particular affliction within the limits of a religious world-view has sometimes resulted in an understanding of these things as an out-working of diabolical activity, often mediated through a human agent. The Salem witch trials of the seventeenth century are a case in point.

Science fiction is replete with stories concerning the nature of reality, the order of things and our perception of such order. Most of these tales can be seen to have their roots in Plato's famous analogy of the cave in which what is taken for reality is revealed to be nothing more than a shadow when the viewer leaves the cave and enters the light of day. A more socio-cultural template for such stories can be found in Samuel Johnson's *The History of Rasselas* (1759) in which the eponymous hero escapes from the idyllic but intellectually stultifying reality of his home in the mountains to discover a harsher but ultimately more stimulating world outside. These stories have been retold countless times within the genre of SF and represent attempts to focus our attention upon issues relating to our perception of the world in which we find ourselves and the alteration in that perception which accompanies growing up and the concomitant increase in experience. Sometimes such changes in perception are couched in terms of the Judaeo-Christian understanding of humanity's exile from paradise subsequent to gaining the for-bidden knowledge of good and evil. More often such perceptual changes or 'paradigm shifts' are presented in a more positive mode as a freedom from ignorance and misapprehension, a questioning of the *status quo* or as a natural part of human development. Examples of this can be found in stories such as Arthur C. Clarke's *The City and the Stars* (1956), P. K. Dick's *Time Out of Joint* (1958) and D. F. Galouye's *Dark Universe* (1967), as well as the 1960s *Star Trek* episodes 'The Apple', 'The World is Hollow and I have Touched the Sky', the *Star Trek: The Next Generation* episode 'The Masterpiece Society', and films such as *Zardoz* (1974) and *Logan's Run* (1976).

Invariably the catalyst that triggers the paradigm shift in these stories, a change from one world-view to another, is the introduction of an element which begins to break down the sense of order previously accepted by default. The existentialist philosopher Karl Jaspers describes such an experience as a 'boundary experience' – that is, one in which one's very understanding of the order and meaning of reality are brought into question. Near-death experiences are the most common and most readily understood instances of such boundary situations. The old adage that there are no atheists in the trenches speaks of a fundamental human desire for order and meaning in the face of imminent dissolution and oblivion. When the regular pattern of our lives is disrupted, whether at a level of minor inconvenience such as the cancelling of our usual train, or at a more profound level such as the loss of a loved one, it brings this otherwise unconscious and unconsidered pattern into focus. Often we only recognise the nature and significance of order when such order breaks down.

In the *Star Trek* episode 'The World is Hollow and I have Touched the Sky' an entire culture is found to be living within what appears to be a hollowed-out asteroid known as Yonada. It is only when this asteroid is discovered to be on a collision course with a populated planet that their world-view is challenged – along with the religion that supports it – and the true nature of the 'world', that it is in fact a malfunctioning space vessel, is revealed.

In R. Matheson's novel *I Am Legend* (1954), a plague transforms all but Robert Neville into vampires. During the course of this fascinating novel we see Neville's world-view slowly unravel in spite of his best attempts to maintain it via routine and familiar objects.

He was putting the food on his plate when he stopped and his eyes moved quickly to the clock. Six-twenty-five today. Ben Cortman was shouting.

'Come out, Neville!'

Robert Neville sat down with a sigh and began to eat.

He sat in the living room, trying to read. He'd made himself a whiskey and soda at his small bar and he held the cold glass as he read a physiology text. From the speaker over the hallway door, the music of Schoenberg was playing loudly.

Not loudly enough, though. He still heard them outside, their murmuring and their walking about and their cries, their snarling and fighting among themselves. Once in a while a rock or brick thudded off the house. Sometimes a dog barked.

And they were all there for the same thing.[3]

In a powerful ironic twist, the story ends with Neville being recast in the role of the monster who finally understands that in this new world order he has become the terror that stalks and destroys the fearful vampiric populace as it sleeps.

They all stood looking up at him with their white faces. He stared back. And suddenly he thought, I'm the abnormal one now. Normalcy was a majority concept, the standard of many not the standard of just one man. Abruptly that realization joined with what he saw on their faces – awe, fear, shrinking horror – and he knew that they were afraid of him. To them he was some terrible scourge they had never seen, a scourge even worse than the disease they had come to live with. He was an invisible spectre who had left for evidence of his existence the bloodless bodies of their loved ones. And he understood what they felt and did not hate them.[4]

Are we significant?

If the human desire for order is strong then the quest for meaning is equally so, if not stronger. While the quest for order has to do with a concern for pattern and consistency throughout the universe, the quest for *meaning* speaks to our desire for existential significance. Nobody would wish to believe themselves to be living a meaningless life – to entertain such a thought is to court apathy and despair at best and self-destruction at worst. For this reason we seek out sources of significance, activities, beliefs and relationships which serve to provide our existences with meaning. Where we choose to look for our life's meaning depends greatly upon our own personal understanding of the nature of the world in which we find ourselves and the beliefs that inform that understanding. Whether we are inherently significant or need to have significance attributed to us by virtue of some activity or other relies upon our anthropological perspective, upon our convictions concerning the nature of human existence. For example, within the Judaeo-Christian tradition human beings are said to have been created in the divine image, as the high point in the divine plan to create a world. The implication of such a view is to regard all human life as innately valuable and of inestimable significance.

The meaning of a human being understood as being created in, or (according to some theologians) destined to become, the divine image is established by virtue of its image-bearing nature prior to any activity on the part of any particular human individual. This, as we noted in a previous chapter, reflects an *essentialist* view of human being, one which regards humanness and its distinctive value as something we possess from birth, and possibly even earlier, irrespective of any external factors. While a variety of Christian theologians such as Augustine and Reformers such as John Calvin regard the image of God as in some way compromised or even effaced as a result of humanity's fall from grace, there are few who would deny that our humanity is a function of our creatureliness, of our being created by and in relationship with a God who intended something specific through this act of creation. Even the Protestant theologian Karl Barth, who famously declared the image of God in humanity as 'totally annihilated',[5] wishes to maintain a notion of human value and distinctiveness on the basis of humanity's unavoidable encounter with God specifically in Jesus Christ the God/Man. What underlies this idea of essential humanity is the notion of *normativity*, that is to say that there is a mode of existence that is right and proper for human beings.

Writers of SF – in spite of any expectation that hard science is their primary concern – seem to have a fondness for the notion that human beings are more than meets the eye, that they are, or at least possess, some manner of ephemeral, perhaps even immortal, essence. The popularity of this premise within the genre is the starting point for a variety of tales concerning body-swapping, life after death and the inhabiting of alternative realities.

In his short story 'This Life and Later Ones' George Zebrowski – an SF author well known for his treatment of philosophical and religious themes – addresses the issue of whether there is a human essence which might persist after the death of the body.[6] The story begins with the presentation of three choices that face humanity in some near future: 'death with nothing after; death with the religious or mystical hope of a new existence; or translation into a manufactured afterlife.'[7] The rest of the story, told by a man whose ninety-year-old father is about to die, tells of a technique whereby those on the brink of death might have their essence – for want of a better term – transferred into a computer-generated afterlife.

He went the same week. They used the actual atoms of his brain to form the transfer pattern, for metaphysical reasons of conserving identity, they said; otherwise we might consider him only a copy of himself. I went to the warehouse and saw row

upon row of solid-state modules housing the electronic dead in
what amounted to old age homes beyond the grave.[8]

However, the construction of a convincing world, let alone a
paradisaical afterlife, proves to be problematic and the 'sub-
scribers', as they are referred to, soon begin to complain about
the lack of detail in their new world. Zebrowski paints a
chilling image of those inhabiting this virtual afterlife being
visited by their loved ones who can do little more than gaze
into this shadow world through a viewing screen. As the
departed no longer possess physical bodies, with all the
attendant glands and hormones, they soon begin to lose
the capacity to feel emotions, merely remembering how those
feelings once felt. Such a life is presented as hardly worth
sustaining:

To make matters worse, there were few psychologists in the
field of identity transfer – you died and woke up in another
place, where your experience of a well-made world told you
that this was no world at all. It had been made by an idiot
god, or a devil attempting to mimic reality . . . 'It is a big
change,' Felix, the ace programmer, explained to me. 'We
didn't understand how big until we pulled in a few psycho-
biologists. It seems that the loss of the body's emotion-
producing system begins to show up. The brain tries to go on
as before, out of habit and memory, but then coldness sets
in.'[9]

It is debated whether or not to allow the occupants of this
virtual afterlife direct access to the software tools used to
create their world, in effect to give them godlike powers over
their environment; however, this idea is rejected on the
grounds that human beings seem to require limits and that
the old adage that absolute power corrupts absolutely may
well prove to be accurate.[10] Eventually it is decided that the
writer's father be transferred into a 'hardbody', a cybernetic
replica of the deceased body as it appeared in its prime: 'Some
people liked the overt Cartesian mind-body dualism. They

could drive their new bodies from the head. I suppose it reminded them of their car.'[11] The story ends with the profoundly disturbing revelation that although the writer's father has been transferred from the virtual world into the cybernetic body, there still exists a residual trace of the father's data within that world, a ghost of a ghost who cannot be erased and who implores his son to get him out.

Stories such as this one focus upon the notion of a human essence which transcends the physical world and the physical body and yet for all that there is still a wish to emphasise the significance of physicality for meaningful human existence. Whether it is possible, ultimately, to reduce this essence to a form of data which can be transmitted and stored in something other than its original body is a question that has yet to receive a definitive answer. Certainly within the Christian tradition there is an understanding of the survival of the essential person after the death of the body. Where this 'essence' goes, and by what means, is not, to my mind, made clear within the tradition, though it is clear that it is of value to God and thus deserves to be preserved. Of course not everyone accepts an essentialist view of human nature and many remain unconvinced of humanity's transcendental value as creatures of a divine creator. In this case human significance and value must be attributed to human beings upon different grounds.

Human being, value and rights

During the conflict in Kosovo terms such as 'human rights' and 'crimes against humanity' were bandied about by the media as if these were unproblematic concepts. The former Chilean dictator General Pinochet was, at the same time, in fear of extradition to Spain where he would be tried for mass murder and, once again, crimes against humanity. That human beings are significant and valuable is something that the international community, if one can speak of such a thing, seems to wish to assert and support with the rule of law and indeed with military intervention. Nevertheless, the source of this value, the foundation for utterances, actions and policies concerning human rights requires to be identified if international law and common morality are to have any real significance beyond taste and sentiment.

In his recent book describing the development of the notion of crimes against humanity, Geoffrey Robertson points out that the notion of human rights lacked any real power prior to the holocaust of the second world war.

The notion that 'rights' might belong to anyone, anywhere, as a human inheritance was ridiculed by nineteenth-century philosophers and when the majority of Western powers agreed to outlaw slavery, this was attributed to shared moral generosity rather than to any recognition of an inalienable individual right not to be held in bondage or servitude. It dawned on no political leader, even after the carnage of the First World War, that international institutions might tell states how to treat their nationals – the League of Nations and the Permanent Court of International Justice were untroubled by 'human rights' until Hitler rendered them irrelevant. At this point, the individual had no rights in international law – a subject which dealt with treaties and agreements between states and was completely inaccessible to their citizens.[12]

The philosophers he has in mind here are principally the Utilitarian Jeremy Bentham and Karl Marx. It was Bentham who famously referred to natural rights as 'nonsense upon stilts' and feared that such language was deployed for the sole purpose of attacking the aristocracy and would inevitably give rise to the social chaos witnessed during the French Revolution. Furthermore he argued that the potential sources of these alleged natural rights were vague and unreliable at best, issuing either from God, and thus being ultimately inaccessible – the Bible notwithstanding – or from nature and therefore being open to interpretation. Marx's critique of the 'rights of man' focuses upon what he saw as the bourgeois individualism inherent within the notion: ' . . . the so-called rights of man . . .

are nothing but the rights of egotistic man separated from other men and from their community.'[13]

What is of particular interest here is Robertson's observation that it was H. G. Wells who brought about the revival of the idea of human rights in the early part of the twentieth century and helped to set the agenda for the formation of the United Nations and its Charter in 1944. Wells argued for 'a fundamental law for mankind throughout the world' and along with a small number of like-minded friends such as J. B. Priestley and A. A. Milne – who, by the way, also wrote in the fields of SF and fantasy – went on to produce a nine-point declaration of human rights. This remarkable, and widely admired, document enshrined a belief in a human being's rights to food, clothing, housing and medical care – in fact all things necessary to 'physical and mental development'. It went on to declare the human right to education and information, along with the protection of person and property, and to denounce the keeping of 'secret dossiers in any administrative department' and the use of torture.

. . . no man shall be subjected to torture, beating or any other bodily punishment, or to imprisonment with such an excess of silence, noise, light or darkness as to cause mental suffering or in infected, verminous or otherwise insanitary quarters.[14]

As laudable – and, to many, self-evident – as this all sounds, the establishing of a declaration of human rights stumbles at the point of universal recognition and adherence. Wells himself was quite adamant that national boundaries ought not to interfere with the sometimes necessary enforcement of these rights.

There was an extraordinary mass of foolish talk after 1918 about not interfering in the internal affairs of this, that or the other member of the League of Nations. It is time we recognised fully that the making of any lethal weapon larger than what we may require for the control of big animals, is a matter of universal concern . . .[15]

Yet, in spite of the influence of Wells' work upon the high profile given to human rights within the UN Charter, this did not prevent the inclusion of Article 2(7), a rule that, according to Geoffrey Robertson, has effectively crippled the notion of international human rights for much of this century.

Nothing contained in the present charter shall authorize the United Nations to intervene in matters which are essentially within the domestic jurisdiction of any State or shall require the members to submit such matters to settlement under the present Charter.[16]

This particular conundrum – how to exercise respect for human rights while preserving equal respect for sovereignty and cultural diversity – is one that is visited again and again within the genre of SF. Ever since Jules Verne's Captain Nemo took the administration of international justice into his own hands with his submarine *Nautilus* in the 1870 novel *Twenty Thousand Leagues Under the Sea*, there have been no shortage of national, international and extra-terrestrial vigilantes within the genre. Verne himself revisited the theme in his 1886 work *The Clipper of the Clouds*, in which Robur confronts the world from a powerful airship rather than a submarine. And, as we saw earlier (page 76), in the classic 1951 film *The Day the Earth Stood Still*, the alien ambassador Klaatu presents the people of Earth with an ultimatum: put aside any thoughts of violent expansion beyond your planetary borders or you will be destroyed.

In the *Star Trek* series we find an almost exact correlation with Article 2(7) in the famous, or perhaps infamous, 'Prime Directive' which essentially prohibits intervention within the domestic affairs of other races for whatever reason. The Prime Directive – or 'General Order Number One', as it is sometimes referred to – embodies *Star Trek*'s apparent anti-colonial and anti-militarist philosophy. In creating his utopian view of the future, Gene Roddenberry portrays a 'United Federation of Planets' formed out of mutual co-operation and a shared belief in the sort of liberal humanism encouraged by the Enlightenment. To make the point further, the enlightened and civilised Federation was juxtaposed with the warlike and aggressive Klingon Empire, and, to a lesser extent, the Romulan Empire, whose policy of colonisation via military conquest was a clear, and none too subtle, reflection of Soviet expansionist policies of the 1960s.

In 'Errand of Mercy', the episode of the 1960 *Star Trek* series in which we first encounter the Klingon menace, Captain Kirk and Mr Spock are sent to the planet Organia to warn the primitive inhabitants of the imminent danger of Klingon invasion. To the surprise and frustration of the Federation representatives, the Organians refuse their help and similarly refuse to resist the Klingon occupation forces that eventually arrive. The Organians finally reveal themselves to be superior, almost godlike beings, who have assumed a human appearance for the sake of their 'guest' and now have had enough of the petty and childish squabbles of these two warring factions. The Organians proceed to establish a buffer zone between the two super-powers in which no weapon is permitted to function and then, with no small expression of distaste, they dismiss both parties.

'Errand of Mercy' is an excellent story that illustrates the dangers of technological and ideological paternalism. The Federation is so confident in its moral and technological superiority that it finds it inconceivable that any sane culture should turn down their benevolent offer of aid. The recognition that other cultures might have achieved a level of enlightened civilised existence without excessive use of technology is one that both the fictional Federation and our own technologically developed cultures have found difficult to accept. Similarly, those whose view of reality and human existence is one which attributes value to the non-physical – perhaps to the realm of ideas or emotions, or even to a spiritual reality that transcends the natural world – often find themselves out of sync within a culture that values physical substance and the power to manipulate it above all else.

It would seem that the meaning and value of a human life

is doomed to a relative status depending, in large part, upon accident of birth, so long as the existence of individual sovereign states are understood as determining factors in the definition of that life. If our lives are not to be regarded as transcendentally meaningful then we are forced, in an existential mode, to find meaning wherever we may. While some may choose to invest their day-to-day occupation or their status as parent, lover or member of a community with the task of validating their lives, others may opt for a more violent, antisocial or self-serving route. Any attempt at arbitrating between the various ways in which meaning and significance have been attributed to human existence must surely become a pointless exercise in comparative taste.

Making sense of our world

Making sense of the world, or at least our bit of it, is clearly an ongoing human activity. While a very young child may be initially prepared to engage with the sheer fact of the world – this is a ball, that is a dog, you are a parent – this simple labelling soon gives way to a questioning of the world, to the word 'why?'. From this point on we are never truly satisfied with the simple fact of the world; we wish to interpret it, we want to understand why things are the way they are, we need to feel that, for good or ill, the universe we inhabit makes *sense*. We often find ourselves questioning the universe, asking why certain things have or have not taken place as if there were a reason, an answer to all the 'whys' of the world. We are profoundly dissatisfied with authoritarian or fatalistic responses to our questions. Simply to be told 'because I say so' or even 'just because' is not enough, even for children, although it is often all we are permitted. Senselessness is, I believe, profoundly offensive to the human psyche: senseless destruction, senseless waste, senseless violence are somehow worse than destruction, waste and violence with a purpose. In his novel *Voyage to Venus* (1943), C. S. Lewis provides us

with a chilling account of senseless evil when he describes an
encounter between the hero, Ransom, and the Un-man:

*Hours later the Un-man began to speak. It did not even look in
Ransom's direction; slowly and cumbersomely, as if by some
machinery that needed oiling, it made its mouth and lips
pronounce his name.*

'Ransom,' it said.

'Well?' said Ransom.

*'Nothing,' said the Un-man. He shot an inquisitive glance at
it. Was the creature mad? But it looked, as before, dead rather
than mad, sitting there with head bowed and the mouth a little
open, and some yellow dust from the moss settled in the
creases of its cheeks, and the legs crossed tailor-wise, and
the hands, with their long metallic-looking nails, pressed flat
together on the ground before it. He dismissed the problem from
his mind and returned to his own uncomfortable thoughts.*

'Ransom,' it said again.

'What is it?' said Ransom sharply.

'Nothing,' it answered.

*Again there was silence; and again, about a minute later, the
horrible mouth said: 'Ransom!' This time he made no reply.
Another minute and it uttered his name again; and then, like
a minute gun, 'Ransom . . . Ransom . . . Ransom,' perhaps a
hundred times.*

'What the Hell do you want?' he roared at last.

*'Nothing,' said the voice . . . If the attack had been of some
more violent kind it might have been easier to resist. What
chilled and almost cowed him was the union of malice with
something nearly childish. For temptation, for blasphemy, for
a whole battery of horrors, he was in some sort prepared: but
hardly for this petty, indefatigable nagging as of a nasty little
boy at a preparatory school. Indeed no imagined horror could
have surpassed the sense which grew within him as the slow
hours passed, that this creature was, by all human standards,
inside out – its heart on the surface and its shallowness at the
heart. On the surface, great designs and an antagonism to*

Heaven which involved the fate of worlds: but deep within, when every veil had been pierced, was there, after all nothing but black puerility, an aimless empty spitefulness . . .[17]

Natural disasters, such as the earthquake in Turkey that killed thousands in August 1999, tragic deaths, particularly of young children, wars, famines and illnesses along with incidents of good luck, success and survival against the odds all elicit the question why? That such things should occur without reason, that they are the senseless out-workings of a meaningless world is too disturbing a thought to entertain for long. For the universe to call out our name at birth, only to reply with 'nothing' once we answer is a dark thought indeed and one that speaks of an aimlessness to existence that, I would suggest, is difficult to live with.

In our quest for *order* and *meaning* and *sense* we seek to identify our place in the world and to navigate the most appropriate and satisfying path through life towards some manner of final resolution. What we are speaking of here is a belief, perhaps a tacit one, in a purposeful existence, a significant life, a destiny. Human destiny, our purpose and ultimate *telos* or destination is a theme that is considered at length by a variety of philosophical and religious traditions and, not surprisingly, by writers of SF who are uniquely concerned with where humanity might find itself in some distant future. Much depends upon the author's anthropological perspective. 'Just exactly what is a human being?' is a necessary preliminary question that requires an answer before one can tackle questions such as: 'What is best for humanity?' and 'Where are we likely to end up?'

The Christian religious tradition has dealt with the issue of ultimate human destiny at length and in a variety of ways. Classically we find the polarisation between heaven and hell, a divinely instituted utopia for the faithful and eternal damnation and suffering for the infidel. The fourth-century theologian Augustine of Hippo spoke of 'The City of God' – as opposed to 'The Earthly City' – as the realm of God's

authority and rule which is destined to become an eschatological paradise where all things, by the grace of God, are brought
back into harmony with each other, a harmony lost at the fall,
as described in the opening chapters of the book of Genesis.
Augustine is equally convinced of the reality of hell as the
eternal abode of the damned, which represents the eschatological destiny of the unredeemed within 'The Earthly City', the
present reality characterised by toil and suffering. Augustine
thought – and attempted to demonstrate with reference to the
Old Testament – that the whole of human history can be
understood in terms of the relationship and distinction
between the earthly city and the City of God. Those who are
truly saved are caught between the two – citizens of the City
of God, but for the period of their earthly lives living within
the earthly city as pilgrims or aliens.

Whether one accepts such a polarisation depends in large
part upon one's understanding of the divine character and of
course human nature. Is the god that one worships, within
any religion, the kind of being who would, for whatever reason,
create a hell, a place of eternal punishment and suffering? Are
human beings ultimately responsible for their own destiny or
is the human condition a tragic one characterised by a lack of
power over the givenness of existence, the linear and determined nature of their lives? Is humanity, in the final analysis,
basically good or basically evil? Certainly there is no lack of
evidence to support either perspective. Human beings are
clearly capable of monstrous evil as well as petty selfishness;
nevertheless the human capacity for magnanimity and self-
sacrifice is equally arresting. In Voltaire's *Candide* the eponymous hero asks this question of the academic Martin:

*'Do you think ... that men have always massacred each other,
as they do today, that they have always been false, cozening,
faithless, ungrateful, thieving, weak, inconsistent, mean-
spirited, envious, greedy, drunken, miserly, ambitious, bloody,
slanderous, debauched, fanatic, hypocritical, and stupid?'*[18]

Martin responds that it is as natural for man to be this way as it is for a bird of prey to attack smaller birds – it is in his nature. Of course, to deploy the notion of intractable nature in this way might be seen as excusing humanity for its evils by casting it in the tragic mode, as beings whose behaviour patterns are not within its rational control. In the *Star Trek: Voyager* episode 'Scorpion' the captain of the starship *Voyager* needs to make a decision as to whether or not to join forces with the Borg – a long-time enemy of the Federation – in the face of an even greater threat. The captain's first officer is dubious about the prudence of such an alliance, citing an old story concerning a fox and a scorpion. The scorpion, unable to swim, asks the fox if it might carry him across a river. The fox, wary of the scorpion, refuses, arguing, not unreasonably, that the scorpion would sting him. The scorpion assures the fox that it would not be in his best interest to sting the fox as if he did the fox would drown, taking the scorpion with him. The fox succumbs to this logic and begins to ferry the scorpion across the river. However, halfway across the river the scorpion does indeed sting the fox and as the fox begins to die he turns to the scorpion and says 'Why did you do that? Now we'll both die', to which the scorpion replied, 'I couldn't help it, it's my nature.'

As we have already noted, with the Enlightenment's increasing understanding of the world as a natural machine governed by ascertainable laws, human beings themselves began to be seen in a new light. Rather than being understood as dependent/contingent creatures that needed to look beyond themselves for meaning and significance, humanity became redefined in secular terms as the centre of reality, as the source of all truth and value. It was reason, properly utilised, that would enable humanity to cut through the fog of superstition, traditional prejudices and other confusions so as to provide a true understanding of the mechanism called nature. Laws could be identified and religious/mythical explanations could be dispensed with. Human being was elevated to an epistemically privileged position, with regard to knowledge, where it was possible to make definitive pronouncements concerning objective truths.

Furthermore, it was now possible for human beings to examine and understand themselves, to address the human question armed with the new tools of scientific analysis and thence to begin to create a uniquely human destiny. It is during this period that we begin to see the development of what would come to be known as the social sciences. Human beings were no longer regarded as creatures of God by the prevailing world-view but as products of nature and their environment. This is very important when seen in the context of the emerging natural sciences. For, if it is indeed possible to master the natural world and to engineer our environment, and if moreover we are nothing more or less than products of our environment, blank slates to be written on, without even the comfort of natural rights to help define our place in the world, then it follows that we ought to be able to remake ourselves via a process of environmental manipulation and social conditioning. This of course is precisely what we have been attempting to do ever since socially, politically and biologically, to create a new identity for ourselves and concomitantly a new destiny. Indeed, both the United States of America and the former Soviet Union can be seen – more obviously with the latter – as the results of competing Enlightenment utopian projects.

Things can only get better

One of the key elements in the Enlightenment's optimistic understanding of humanity and its potential is summed up in the idea of *progress*. Despite the present attitude that the doctrine of progress is a self-evident one and that it is (a) a good thing, and (b) inevitable, it is in fact a comparatively new idea.

The Judaeo-Christian tradition, for example, speaks not of a steady progression and improvement but of a number of 'states' of human being: Original Perfection, Fall, New

Creation. Furthermore, the promised new creation, the Christian utopia, is not the product of human development but the work of Christ and a gift of divine grace. The Classical Greek tradition – rediscovered during the Renaissance – spoke of a cyclical process: a golden age, followed by a silver age, then an iron age and then back again to a golden age. Renaissance humanists, therefore, tended to look to a lost golden age in the past rather than forward to some new paradise never before experienced by human beings.

It was during the seventeenth century that a belief began to develop in the potential superiority of the present over the past, sometimes referred to as the 'Quarrel of the Ancients and the Moderns' or the 'Battle of the Books'. In the first instance this was largely a literary issue: can a modern writer produce a work equal to or even superior to one of the ancients? At this time novelty was considered to be trivial and reference to past authority was often the final arbiter in all intellectual disagreements. It was commonly held that the writings of great thinkers such as Plato, Homer and Augustine – not to mention the Bible – could not be superseded or improved upon and that all subsequent productions ought properly to be seen as commentary upon the work of the greats of the past. However, by the early eighteenth century attitudes began to change as the Enlightenment's inexorable challenging of traditional authorities began to gain greater acceptance.

In 1750 the French philosopher Turgot produced a complete doctrine of progress in his work *On the Successive Advances of the Human Mind*. His friend and disciple Condorcet developed this doctrine into a view of a utopian future, in which humanity would ultimately achieve 'natural salvation' – that is to say, immortality by natural means and as the product of rational endeavour. We must remind ourselves at this point that Darwinian evolutionary theory would not arrive until the nineteenth century, thus there was no biological understanding of progress from a lower to a higher form of life intended here, but simply a profound belief in the ability of human reason to find the answer to human mortality. As we have already noted in a previous chapter, this is very much at the heart of Shelley's *Frankenstein* story.

In the view of the Enlightenment, progress is brought about by a combination of reason and cultural and social engineering. Education was therefore of great importance in all ideas of social reform. Indeed, so powerful was this notion of progress towards an ideal society that the classical theological liberalism of the nineteenth century, typified by thinkers such as Albrecht Ritschl and Adolf von Harnack, identified the 'Kingdom of God' as an earthly utopia, the end-point of human progress.

In very general terms, SF is polarised with respect to its presentation of human destiny, opting either for a glorious utopian image of an almost godlike humanity or for its obverse, a dystopian view of a devastated and bestial humanity often occupying the crumbling remains of its world. In the main human destiny is seen to be in the hands of humanity itself, in such a way that we are portrayed as essentially good, rational beings progressing along the road to enlightenment or alternatively as a collection of petty self-serving individuals who ultimately destroy themselves, or at least their civilisation, out of a combination of greed and stupidity.

Utopia

The word *utopia* actually means 'no place' in Greek – in that it intended to speak of an unrealisable ideal – and was most famously used by Thomas More in his 1516 publication of the same name. In this work More attempts to describe an imaginary island, the inhabitants of which live a perfect and harmonious existence. Of course the notion of an ideal society whose members live a perfect and wholly satisfying life is one of great antiquity. Plato's most famous work *The Republic*, written some time during the fourth century BC, gives an account of the perfect state, one founded upon the four cardinal virtues of wisdom, courage, discipline and justice. Wisdom is seen as issuing from the rulers, that is to say the philosophers, courage from the auxiliaries, that is the military or executive branch of the government, and self-discipline speaks of the agreement by the individual members of the state to acknowledge both the ruling class and their own place in society. Justice, in many ways, represents the lynch-pin of the Platonic state and is summed up by Plato in this way:

Well then, listen, and see if you think I'm talking sense. I believe
justice is the requirement we laid down at the beginning as
of universal application when we founded our state, or else
some particular form of it. We laid down, if you remember,
and have often repeated, that in our state one man was to do
one job, the job he was naturally most suited for ... And
further, we have often heard it said and often said ourselves
that justice consists in minding your own business and not
interfering with other people.[19]

In the episode called 'The Masterpiece Society' from *Star Trek: The Next Generation*, the crew of the *Enterprise* encounter a closed 'utopian' society who reluctantly call upon them for help. This society is the product of genetic manipulation by its founders who had planned to engineer the ideal human community in which every individual is genetically 'programmed' to serve the needs of the whole. The leader of the community puts it like this: 'I've been bred to fill this specific role, we grow up knowing exactly what our society needs from us, what we are expected to do.' One of the *Enterprise* officers comments: 'That must take some of the fun out of it', to which the leader replies:

'Not at all. My entire psychological make-up tells me that I was
born to lead. I am exactly what I would choose to be. Think
of it another way. Are there still people in your society who
have not yet discovered who they really are or what they were
meant to do with their lives? They may be in the wrong job,
they may be writing bad poetry or worse they may be great poets
working as labourers never to be discovered. That does not
happen here.'[20]

That a person should both know their place and purpose and be content with it has been a staple utopian theme. The Judaeo-Christian account of Adam and Eve's fall from grace and consequent exile from paradise is seen to be, at least in part, the result of dissatisfaction with their place in the scheme of things, a desire to be something other than they were, to be like God. The result of their fall was to plunge them into an alternative, broken existence characterised by toil and pain, an existence in which their intended harmony with others and the environment was disrupted. An acceptance of this broken, dysfunctional world as fallen humanity's proper place introduces an anti-utopian element within Christian theology, most notable in the works of Augustine. For Augustine, human beings now live a penal existence in a world that punishes them with its harsh conditions for life. Furthermore, Augustine famously advocates a form of political and social quietism founded upon the belief that change for the better is simply not possible in a world orientated towards human punishment by the will of God: 'as far as this life of mortals is concerned, which is spent and ended in a few days, what does it matter under whose government a dying man lives, if they who govern do not force him to impiety and iniquity?'[21]

Many well-known figures have written about the idea of utopia. Examples are Augustine of Hippo's *City of God*, Francis Bacon's *New Atlantis* (1627), Tommaso Campanella's *City of the Sun*, Samuel Butler's *Erewhon* (1872), William Morris' *News from Nowhere* (1891), H. G. Wells' *Modern Utopia* (1905), *Men Like Gods* (1923), *The Shape of Things to Come* (1933) and B. F. Skinner's *Walden Two* (1948).

Utopian perspectives within the genre of SF have ranged from the noble-savage scenario in which humanity, having abandoned technology, opts for a simple, pastoral, lifestyle, to the shining, clean-lined techno wonderland of *Star Trek*, in which, as an exercise of the rational will, humanity is seen as having overcome its baser instincts, focusing its attentions upon self-improvement and the betterment of the species. Often, utopia is achieved by way of socio-political reform coupled with advanced technology; at other times, however, utopian conditions are achieved by virtue of a fundamental evolutionary transformation of the biology of a species.

In *The Time Machine*, H. G. Wells presents us with two unpalatable prospects for human destiny: the Eloi, simple-minded, non-aggressive but stagnant humanity, and the Morlocks, bestial, cannibalistic machine-users who live beneath the earth in the bomb shelters of the last nuclear war. Although the Eloi are, on balance, presented as good and the Morlocks as evil, there is little to choose between the desirability of humanity destined for a life either as mindless cattle or as subterranean monsters.

In most instances utopias are presented not as aspirational images but rather as warnings against uniformity and stagnation. Who is to decide what shape a utopia ought to take? What is the ideal life for human beings? In answer to the first question, Plato would say the philosophers, Wells the technocrats and Skinner the social scientists. As to what constitutes the perfect life this too is open to a variety of responses, perhaps as many as there are individual human beings multiplied by the many changes that each individual human being undergoes throughout the course of their life. In the introduction to *The Faber Book of Utopias*, John Carey makes this important observation:

Anyone who is capable of love must at some time have wanted the world to be a better place, for we all want our loved ones to live free from suffering, injustice and heartbreak. Those who construct utopias build on that universal human longing.
What they build may, however, carry within it its own potential for crushing or limiting human life.
  This is the dilemma that confronts all utopian projects. They aim at a new world, but must destroy the old.[22]

Feminist-resourced utopias, for example, clearly aim at destroying the old world, which is seen as being founded upon patriarchy and the marginalisation of women. In her 1915 novel *Herland*, Charlotte Perkins Gilman presents us with a

feminist utopia of parthenogenic women (i.e. capable of reproduction without fertilisation) – the men having died out
thousands of years ago. These women live in a perfectly bal-
anced classless society in which all the baser qualities,
associated with male-dominated societies, such as greed and
aggression, are not to be found. Furthermore, while the bearing
and raising of children is seen to be of major significance to
the community, the notion of a child 'belonging' to any one
woman or group of women has given way to an understanding
of the child as being mothered by the entire community.

The notion that family and parental bonds are antithetical
to a true utopia is not a new one. Plato, in his *Republic*,
made a similar point, arguing that the state ought to be made
responsible for the upbringing of children – weeding out the
weak in the process – and that it were best if children grew
up not knowing who their parents were so as to avoid harmful
parental influence. In *The Dialectic of Sex*[23] the feminist
theorist Shulamith Firestone argues passionately that it is precisely the debilitating effects of reproductive biology that have
given rise to the oppression and marginalisation of women.
Concomitantly, any technique, social or biotechnological, that
might serve to free women from the tyranny of motherhood
is to be embraced.

The idea that sex and reproduction serve only to unbalance
a society, particularly when the reproductive function is
located in only one gender, is explored in Ursula Le Guin's
1969 novel *The Left Hand of Darkness*. In this story a human
male ethnologist visits Gethen, a planet whose dominant
species are androgynous and who take on either male or female
characteristics and functions as part of a natural biological
cycle. In *The Wanderground* (1979) by Sally Miller Gearhart,
a future is envisaged in which women exist as renegades living
outside of the male-dominated cities. As a result of their close-
ness to nature and their freedom from all things masculine
these women have developed telepathic abilities and are portrayed as peaceful and compassionate. Their attitude to men
is to see them as irredeemably violent: 'They are driven . . .

Driven in their own madness to destroy themselves and us and any living thing . . . Theirs is the madness of power.'[24]

Perhaps surprisingly, given its orientation to the future, full-blown utopianism has had rather a short history within the genre of SF. Apart from H. G. Wells – whose utopianism was challenged by both C. S. Lewis in *That Hideous Strength* and E. M. Forster in *The Machine Stops* (1909) – the only other thorough-going utopian of the genre would appear to be Hugo Gernsback, the man who invented the term 'science fiction'[25]. Gernsback, as has already been noted, was an avid evangelist for science and the new technologies. In the pulp magazines that he edited during the 1920s, such as *Modern Electrics*, Gernsback wrote predictive stories about the great scientific utopia that was to come, the most notable being 'Ralph 124C 41+' (1925). In this way utopianism, speculation about a better place, can be seen as giving way to the more familiar 'euchronianism', speculation about a better time.[26] However, suspicion concerning science and technology, coupled with the general disillusionment with human nature subsequent to the first world war, led writers of SF to take a more cynical view of the future and concentrate their attentions upon dystopian warnings of things to come, Aldous Huxley's *Brave New World* (1932) being a seminal example of this. Similarly, within Christian theology the liberal optimism of the late nineteenth and early twentieth centuries, which led to a reformulation of the idea of the kingdom of God in terms of an earthly utopia, gave way to the neo-orthodoxy of thinkers such as Karl Barth. Barth – drawing on both Augustine and the sixteenth-century Reformers – rejected any notion of a bright new future ushered in by enlightened humanity in favour of a return to the more classical understanding of the depravity of humanity and the hope for a divinely established apocalyptic kingdom.

Dystopia

Dystopian images – that is, the obverse of utopian – since Shelley's *Frankenstein*, have often focused upon the inability of humanity to adequately control its creations. Machines, weapons of mass destruction, chemical and biological agents of every kind and even nature itself have all conspired against humanity to bring about its downfall. Often, the Baconian maxim 'knowledge is power' – an aphorism expressing the belief that scientific knowledge of the natural world would provide humanity with coercive power over that world – is tacitly explored within dystopian tales of technological power vested in a minority élite who use this power to enhance their own standing at the expense of the majority. This is a theme that is considered in H. G. Wells' *First Men in the Moon* (1901) – albeit with reference to the alien Selenites – but also in Bertrand Russell's 1924 work *Icarus, or The Future of Science*, as well as D. H. Keller's *The Revolt of the Pedestrians* (1928), S. F. Wright's *The New Gods Lead* (1932) and, notably, Kurt Vonnegut's *Player Piano* (1952). During the latter part of the twentieth century, particularly within the so-called 'cyberpunk' sub-genre, the relationship between technological superiority and political power has been acknowledged almost without question as a backdrop to other apparently more important story elements rather than as one in its own right.

While proto-cyberpunk novels such as Alfred Bester's *Tiger, Tiger*[27] (1953) and John Brunner's *The Shockwave Rider* (1975) present us with a hero, or in Bester's case an anti-hero, who confronts the empowered establishment and ultimately transforms its dystopian product, the central characters – one resists using the term 'hero' here – in recent cyberpunk are rarely out to change the system but simply to survive within it. The character of Case in William Gibson's *Neuromancer* (1984) is seen from the outset of the novel to be at the mercy of greater powers that he cannot hope to understand, let alone match. Peter Nicholls, in his entry on William Gibson in the *Encyclo-*

pedia of Science Fiction, puts it very well when he claims that, 'none of the characters of Neuromancer have anything but an eavesdropping relationship to the true roots of power'.[28] This can also be seen in works such as Jack Womack's *Terraplane* (1988), with its world dominated by super-corporations such as Dryco, Neal Stephenson's *Snow Crash* (1992), with its suburbs operating as individual nation states with their own security forces and passport control, Pat Cadigan's *Fools* (1992), with its Brain Police and the widespread trafficking in illegal memories, and Jeff Noon's *Vurt* (1993), with its vivid depiction of a world dominated by the eponymous reality-altering drug Vurt and the mysterious corporations that produce it.

A great deal of contemporary SF's depictions of dystopias are centred on an oppressive multinational or corporate fascism which relies upon economic power for control. The us/them, haves/have-nots divide is symbolised spatially by the élite's occupancy of chrome-and-steel high-rise fortresses, with the masses scurrying around at street level amongst the decay of collapsing city life. The 1926 film *Metropolis*, along with more recent offerings such as *Blade Runner*, *Robocop*, *The City of Lost Children* and *The Fifth Element*, vividly captures this sense of a two-tiered society in images which portray fantastic opulence for the few and a life of struggle for the rest.

Often, although as we saw earlier, increasingly rarely since the 1980s, there is within this kind of SF a juxtaposing of the corporate and the individual where it is the creativity, flexibility and charisma of the individual person which finally brings the system down. John Brunner's novel *Shockwave Rider* is a case in point, as is the Film *Rollerball* and the 1960s cult television series *The Prisoner*. In effect these individuals take on a messianic role in their conflict with an inhuman system and their preaching of and ushering in of a new order.

There are numerous examples of SF stories utilising the Armageddon scenario – a particularly popular theme since Hiroshima. Often this device provides the writer with the opportunity to start society again from scratch according to some ideal principle or to reflect on the folly of present human behaviour. Notable examples are Wells' *The Time Machine* (1895), and *The Star* (1897), M. P. Shiel's *The Purple Cloud* (1901), E. Shanks' *The People of the Ruins* (1920), P. Wylie and E. Balmer's *When Worlds Collide* (1933, film version 1951), Alfred Bester's *Adam and No Eve* (1941), Judith Merril's *Shadow on the Hearth* (1950), Walter Miller's *A Canticle for Leibowitz* (1955–7), James Blish's *We All Die Naked* (1969), Kurt Vonnegut's *Galapagos* (1985), J. K. Morrow's *This is the Way the World Ends* (1986) and Greg Bear's *Blood Music* (1998).

In the deeply disturbing short story 'I Have No Mouth and I Must Scream' (1967), Harlan Ellison explores not only the consequences of nuclear war but also our relationship with the technologies that serve us. His 'creature' – unlike Shelley's – is the insane supercomputer AM, which has forced the last five human beings to live a tortured existence within its hellish innards.

We had given AM sentience. Inadvertently, of course, but sentience nonetheless. But it had been trapped. AM was not God, he was a machine. We had created him to think, but there was nothing it could do with that creativity. In rage, in frenzy, the machine had killed the human race, almost all of us, and still it was trapped. AM could not wander, AM could not wonder, AM could not belong. He could merely be. And so, with the innate loathing that all machines had always held for the weak, soft creatures who had built them, he had sought revenge. And in paranoia, he had decided to reprieve five of us, for a personal, everlasting punishment that would never serve to diminish his hatred . . . that would merely keep him reminded, amused, proficient at hating man. Immortal, trapped, subject to any torment he could devise for us from the limitless miracles at his command.[29]

As I write we are only a few months away from the beginning of the twenty-first century and the new millennium. While it is difficult to ascertain exactly why this is the case, there seems to be, within popular culture, a sense of expectation associated with this event. There are those who expect the world to end and those who expect a new golden age of peace and harmony, those who expect the burgeoning new technologies to further enhance our lives and those who expect the proliferation of cybernetic and biotechnological industries to further compromise our humanity and damage our environment. As we have seen, these are by no means new hopes and fears but ones which, in some form or another, have concerned humanity in its quest for meaning and significance for centuries.

John Carey makes the point that all utopian projects are united in their quest to 'eliminate real people' and I am inclined to agree. It is, after all, real people who constitute the societies that utopians wish to replace. Human beings – belief in a normative essence notwithstanding – are not easily standardised and thus tend to resist prescribed models of thought and behaviour. Indeed, attempts at such standardisation, often founded upon nationalistic, ideological or eugenic (controlled breeding) grounds, have given rise to some of the most monstrous dystopias imaginable. Whether evolution, genetic manipulation or cybernetics will serve to reinvent humanity remains to be seen; we may indeed be destined for a 'Borg-like' collective existence where each individual is an indistinguishable part of a greater whole, acting with one mind and one will. The consenus of SF is that this would be a bad thing, that individuality is something to be cherished and fought for in the face of all the Daleks, Cybermen and Borg. However, and as cyberpunk authors such as William Gibson have shown us, a destiny in which humanity becomes more and more fragmented and privatised in an increasingly hostile world also has little to recommend it. On the last track of the Eagles' 1976 album *Hotel California*, there is the lyric:

> *They call it paradise,*
> *I don't know why.*

Call some place paradise,
kiss it goodbye.

Perhaps Augustine is right and this world is inevitably hostile to us and thus any attempt at improvement is a wasted one. Perhaps, on the other hand, it is the very attempt rather than any actual utopian outcome that is important.

Elsewhere I have argued that humanity might best be understood in terms of 'coadunacy', the relational dynamic which takes place between distinct others, between the 'I' and the 'you'.[30] If this is the case then perhaps utopia is best understood not in terms of a better place or a better time but rather of a better relationship, be that with other people, the environment or even God.

5
Where Do We Belong?

While at first sight this might sound like a rather facile observation, one of the major defining characteristics of humanity is that it is 'somewhere' rather than 'nowhere', that it exists at a particular time and in a particular place. The existentialist philosopher Martin Heidegger speaks of this in terms of *situatedness*, our actual presence in history, our being 'here'.

How we relate to our surroundings and how this relatedness affects who we are and how we engage with others is an issue that has increased in significance in proportion to our ability to structure our own environment. SF writers have had a great deal to say on this topic: by placing humanity within a variety of situations and contexts they have sought to explore the relationship between human beings and the places in which they live. Over-populated urban jungles, idyllic pastoral settings, harsh desert worlds, virtual realities and environments so alien that they may only be partially experienced via the human senses – in our imaginations we have inhabited them all and they have spoken to us of our unavoidable connection with our own place.

What I propose to do here is to provide some background information on notions such as place, situatedness and indwelling so that we might better understand what is under consideration when we speak of human being as determined by place. Alongside this we shall consider some of the ways in which the genre of SF has sought to bring into focus humanity's unique relationship with its context.

Our situation

Clearly humanity does not exist within a vacuum; we are influenced by the world we live in and we in turn affect that world. Changes in temperature, in seasons, in the atmosphere we breath and the food we eat link us intimately with our environment. Indeed, in our utilisation of tools and our being located in a particular place, we often extend our perception of the immediate self beyond our bodies to incorporate the object or location in question; we become part of a place as it becomes part of us.

This notion of 'situatedness' has received some very valuable consideration from within the post-modern, post-critical and phenomenological schools of thought. In the work of the post-modern philosopher Emmanuel Levinas we find the notion of *habitation*,[1] while the philosopher of science Michael Polanyi makes use of the notion of *indwelling*.[2] Each of them is trying to articulate a view of humanness that incorporates an understanding of our living in an environment, existing in a place, being somewhere. In my view, we find one of the clearest articulations of this theme of indwelling or embodying in the writings of the philosopher Maurice Merleau-Ponty.

For Merleau-Ponty the individualistic character of much of modern thought since the Enlightenment is simply inadequate to the task of describing and understanding human knowing and experience. For example, one is not made aware of individual stimuli to ears and eyes and nose and skin in a piecemeal fashion, but rather as a composite whole. When we hear a piece of music we do not simply register individual notes but a complex of sounds. The medium for our experience of the world is, of course, the body. Our bodies, argues Merleau-Ponty, are not simply objects in a world alongside other similar atomistic objects, but are rather that which gives form and orientation to our world. Merleau-Ponty speaks of

the body as, ' . . . the darkness needed in the theatre to show
up the performance'.[3]

It is because our bodies are the point of intersection between
our immediate selves and our world, that we may experience
the world at all. Merleau-Ponty is quite adamant that we exist
as persons in a world, within a context, and not within some
neutral objective realm from which we might make objective
judgements founded upon indubitable data – a point similarly
made by Heidegger. He calls us to vacate the illusory domain
of essences, as does Levinas for that matter, from whence we
attempt to grasp the 'pure object which the minds soars over'.
To inhabit such a realm is to distance ourselves from experience so much that we must ask the question – is it still really
our experience? Merleau-Ponty would answer no. Just as the
philosopher and ethicist Mary Midgley points out that we
are bound to our context and become nothing more than a
'shrivelled petal'[4] when removed from it, so too does Merleau-
Ponty stress the absolute human necessity of situatedness, of
belonging somewhere. It goes almost without saying that this
somewhere will never remain static, it can never be seen in
terms of a single unchanging place, but it is always somewhere
– never nowhere.

In Clifford Simak's short story 'Desertion' (1944)[5] we are
told of a survey mission to the planet Jupiter. For the most
part the members of the mission live and work in domed
enclosures on the planet's hostile surface. So inhospitable to
human life is Jupiter's atmosphere that the only way in which
the planet could be colonised is if the human body were con-
verted to a form more appropriate to the alien atmosphere: 'For
man, unprotected and in his natural form, would be blotted out
by Jupiter's terrific pressure of fifteen thousand pounds per
square inch, pressure that made terrestrial sea bottoms seem
a vacuum by comparison.' While the conversion process
appears to be successful – a number of human beings having
been transformed into 'Lopers', the highest form of indigenous
life on the planet – none of the four men sent out of the station
in this new form had ever returned. The base commander,

Fowler, decides that he cannot possibly send any more people to their apparent deaths and yet the project is too important to abandon: he thus elects to be the next person to try the process, and his old dog Towser is brought along for company since the process works on animals too. Upon leaving the station in his new form the first thing that strikes Fowler is the alteration in his perception: 'he had expected a hell of ammonia rain and stinking fumes and the deafening, thundering tumult of the storm . . . He had not expected the lashing downpour would be reduced to drifting purple mist that moved like fleeing shadows over a red and purple sward.' Furthermore, he had not expected his dog to be able to speak with him. This new form would appear to possess not only enhanced senses but also a more efficient brain, which permitted telepathic communication as well as a greater intellectual capacity. Both Fowler and Towser begin to experience the world in a heightened way and to understand the world in a similarly heightened manner. It is at this point that the mystery of the previously transformed humans, those who failed to return, comes into focus:

He stared back at the dome, a tiny black thing dwarfed by the distance. Back there were men who couldn't see the beauty that was Jupiter . . . Men who walked alone, in terrible loneliness, talking with their tongue like Boy Scouts wigwagging out their messages, unable to reach out and touch one another's mind as he reached out and touched Towser's mind. Shut off forever from that personal, intimate contact with other living things.

The sense of perfect engagement with that which is beyond the immediate self, with context and with other persons, is an attractive one and one which in many ways goes against the Western cultural grain, with its emphasis upon individualism as the primary mode of human existence, and control and domination as the primary mode of our engagement with the environment. Simak's story ends with a recognition of the way in which humanity has defined itself over and against others and the world, as Fowler and Towser make the obvious choice:

'I can't go back,' said Towser.
'Nor I,' said Fowler.
'They would turn me back into a dog,' said Towser.
'And me,' said Fowler, 'back into a man.'

The point is that as human beings we belong in and are part of a world that is external to our immediate consciousness and this to such an extent that our abstraction from this world via radical individualism, or absorption in the self or what Levinas calls 'totalism' represents a real reduction in our essential humanity.[6]

*This environment of brute existence and essence is not
mysterious: we never quit it, we have no other environment.
The facts and essences are abstractions: what there is are worlds
and a world and a Being not a sum of facts or a system of
ideas, but the impassibility of meaninglessness or ontological
void ... it is, whatever we may say, this world, this Being that
our life, our science, and our philosophy inhabit.*[7]

In short, we exist within a context with which we are actively engaged and not simply observing. For, ultimately, 'there is no essence, no idea, that does not adhere to a domain of history and of geography'.[8] In a manner reminiscent of Polanyi's understanding of tools as extensions of our bodies – 'we pour ourselves out into them and assimilate them as part of our own existence. We accept them existentially by dwelling in them'[9] – so too does Merleau-Ponty speak of a reconfiguration of our body image in the light of its indwelling a particular environment or object: 'To get used to a hat, a car, or a stick is to be transplanted into them, or conversely, to incorporate them into the bulk of our own body.'[10]

It seems to me that the notion of human situatedness offers a valuable insight into an understanding of humanity as residing not simply within the isolated individual but within the contextual complex comprising of the self and the environment. Moreover, such discussions concerning human inhabitation – as found in Merleau-Ponty, for example – are of considerable relevance when we consider the development of new technologies, particularly in the fields of virtual reality and telepresence, as well as the breakthroughs in cybernetics. The first of these raises issues concerning the effect that a fully convincing, computer-generated virtual reality might have upon our sense of identity; the second relates to the way in which the increasing addition of artificial cybernetic parts might, again, radically alter the way in which we view not only ourselves but human being in general.[11] As we shall see, these themes have been considered, well ahead of schedule, by writers of SF, but before we look at them it is important that we spend a little time considering the question that is central to this chapter: what do we actually mean by the word 'place'?

What is 'place'?

Clearly, alongside the primarily subjective and internalised conception of situatedness, as discussed above, there stands the more concrete and external notion of place, as it is often spoken of by geographers and architects.

To feel a sense of belonging when inhabiting a certain geographical place is an experience common to all of us. The place we refer to as 'home' exerts a unique influence over us, which is not easily transferable to any other object or location. It is part of our very humanity to be 'placed' and to respond to such places in a variety of different ways. Some places, such as the town we grew up in or the church we got married in, hold a special significance for us, while other places are simply background locations for our everyday activities. Yet despite the vast range of our possible responses to particular places, one thing is certain: we are never divorced from the phenomenon of place. Humanity is always located, is always in some place, regardless of the intensity of our involvement with that place. The geographical theorist E. Relph writes, quoting Heidegger:

To be human is to live in a world that is filled with significant places: to be human is to have your place. The philosopher Martin Heidegger declared that a 'place' places man in such a way that it reveals the external bonds of his existence and at the same time the depths of his freedom and reality.[12]

Both our identity and our security are intrinsically bound up with our sense of place. We identify ourselves by referring to the house, street, town in which we live and the country to which we belong.

In the remarkable short story 'The Star of Double Darkness' (1955), Gamel Woolsey[13] – a writer not normally noted for her contribution to SF – provides a haunting and somewhat melancholy treatment of the themes of loneliness and displacement. The story is written in the first person and begins with the rather uncharacteristic SF opening – at least for the 1950s – 'There is no use trying to pretend that space travel is ever a pleasure.' The central character amplifies this by explaining that, while the need to discover new sources of raw materials has forced humanity to travel to the stars, leaving Earth is always a painful experience:

I was leaving Earth, and I love Earth. I am of Earth stock, but I was brought up on Mars, and perhaps that's why I like Earth so much. Mars is beautiful in a way, I suppose, but it's a barren frightening way. What with its dry red and yellow bushes, and its perpetual dust storms, and its queer, superintelligent worms and beetles, I've never liked Mars much. But I love Earth. It's so green and fresh, and safe – anyway, compared to most of the places I go to on my travels. And then it's so beautiful – I can never get used to that – it's so beautiful.

In contrast to this account of Earth, the planet Syncroses – the destination of the current mining expedition – is a world in perpetual darkness, an unknown planet that defies even technological attempts at penetrating its darkness. In such a world one is isolated not only from others but also from any sense of context or environment; any sense of belonging is stripped away.

In the blackness there was a mortal chill of utter loneliness, and suddenly I felt so weak and exhausted that I had to sit down, I couldn't stand any longer. Cold ripples of fear kept breaking over me . . . I was afraid to move, for fear of getting more and more hopelessly lost . . . As I sat there in the black silence, the blackness and the deadly gravity seemed to be sucking me down as if I were being engulfed in a black quagmire . . . I shall go mad, I thought, I can't stand it. I shall go mad.

Woolsey's story ends on an optimistic note with respect to human adaptability. The central character, having been taken to the edge of insanity by the isolation induced by the dark planet Syncroses, miraculously undergoes a change in perception. The planet and its inhabitants begin to come into focus as things felt and experienced in a new way as if by an extra sense that went beyond sight and sound. Elsewhere I have commented upon this aspect of Woolsey's story in this way:

Human adaptability to an alien context and environment is here seen as the only hope of salvation once human ingenuity has failed. We may, as a matter of necessity, find ourselves again and again thrust into impenetrable alien contexts which defy our best attempts at mastery and yet there is hope that while the context may be intractable, we are not. Our ability to be transformed by our environment is our strength, indeed I believe Woolsey to be saying that nothing is ultimately alien to us, no matter how much it may seem to be so. It is this ability to adapt to the unknown that makes it possible to enter the dark and mysterious places despite our reluctance to do so.[14]

The expression of place-related identity has many different levels of emphasis depending upon the sort of self-identification we are seeking to convey. Within the context of immediate locality within a particular street, for example, we might be identified by the name or number of our house. A different identification comes into play when we are supporting a local football team or expressing regional differences or when one's country goes to war. Indeed, were extraterrestrial contact to become a commonplace, a sense of planetary identity would no doubt become relevant. Many SF stories that appear to deal with alien worlds or extraterrestrial visitors to our own world are concerned, at least in part, with the issues of place and belonging – Spielberg's *ET* (1982) was famously concerned with 'phoning' and ultimately going home.

But what exactly is a place? And what constitutes the identity of a place, such that we, as human beings, can and indeed must participate in it?

In his book *Place and Placelessness*, E. Relph usefully identifies a number of different types of space or place. 'Perceptual space', for example, is that space in which we act. It is in and through this space that we have direct contact with the places around us, and in and through which, to make use of a biblical allusion, 'we live and move and have our being'. Perceptual space provides us with the framework within which we define things and settings as close to us or far away from us, crowded or empty, man-made or natural. Certain perceptual spaces constitute places of great personal significance to us. They are the places to which we commit part of ourselves and which, in turn, give themselves up to us in a reciprocal act of identity enhancement. Such perceptual spaces, where personal, are not uniquely private. We may share a public landscape or place as well as experience the intrinsic continuity between your place and mine. G. Matorz expresses the depth of our involvement in perceptual space in this way: 'We do not grasp space only by our senses . . . we live in it, we project our personality into it, we are tied to it by emotional bonds, space is not just perceived . . . it is lived.'[15]

The value and significance that human beings attribute to sheer physical space is brought into sharp focus in a number of SF stories that deal with the theme of overcrowding. In J. G. Ballard's 1961 short story 'Billennium' we are shown a future world where overcrowding has reached such proportions that people spend most of their spare time trying to find more living room, and where the central topic of conversation is space:

'I hear they may reduce the allocation to three and a half meters,' Rossiter remarked.

Ward paused to allow a party of tenants from the sixth floor to pass down the staircase, holding the door to prevent it jumping off its latch. 'So they're always saying,' he commented. 'I can remember that rumour ten years ago.'

'It's no rumour,' Rossiter warned him, 'it may well be necessary soon. Thirty million people are packed into this city now, a million increase in just one year. There's been some pretty serious talk at the housing department.'

Ward shook his head. 'A drastic revaluation like that is almost impossible to carry out . . . Besides, how can you live in just three and a half metres!'[16]

This theme was revisited in Harry Harrison's 1966 story Make Room! Make Room! (subsequently filmed, albeit loosely adapted, as Soylent Green in 1973) as well as in the original Star Trek series episode 'The Mark of Gideon' (1969).

Existential space, argues Relph, is that space which receives its definition and structure from the particular culture to which we belong.[17] The meaning of such space is in a constant state of flux as it undergoes a never-ending process of restructuring as a result of human activities. In short, existential space is that space which is defined by society and experienced by the individual. Such space may be defined as sacred, as in the case of a church, or authoritative, as in the case of a police station or 10 Downing Street or the White House, for instance. A single place may have a variety of significant meanings, some of them competing. Take St Paul's Cathedral in London; is it a place of worship, a tourist attraction or a national monument? It has been argued by various pagan groups that fencing off Stonehenge as a tourist attraction has deprived them of one of their most sacred sites and places of worship. Pilgrimages to sacred sites often continue long after the original events which instilled them with significance have passed into history, if not into myth and legend. Thousands of people every year visit Israel not as a country but as 'The Holy Land'. And at the beginning of the new millennium thousands of people converged on Greenwich, convinced in some way of its millennial significance.

In an amusing but also melancholy tale by Arthur C. Clarke entitled *The Possessed* (1952) we are introduced to a disembodied space-roving race known as the Swarm. This race had travelled through space for millions of years seeking a new home until finally it came across prehistoric Earth. We learn that the Swarm needs to merge with an intelligent host before it can properly inhabit a new world:

It could not guess which of the countless life-forms on this planet would be the heir to the future, and without such a host it was helpless – a mere pattern of electric charges, a matrix of order and self-awareness in a universe of chaos. By its own resources the Swarm had no control over matter, yet once it had lodged in the mind of a sentient race there was nothing that lay beyond its powers.

The Swarm decides to split into two separate beings – a parent and a child. The parent being returns to space to seek out a more promising planet, while the child remains on earth in the hope that an intelligent species might one day evolve that would suit their purpose. It is agreed that the offspring should return to a preordained spot on the Earth's surface at regular intervals and that the parent being would meet it there if and when its search for a better world proved successful. The part of the Swarm that remained on Earth began the task of choosing a host to join with – one that might one day achieve intelligence:

The search was long and the choice difficult, but at last the

Swarm selected its host. Like rain sinking into thirsty soil, it entered the bodies of certain small lizards and began to direct their destiny.

It was an immense task, even for a being which could never know death. Generation after generation of the lizards was swept into the past before there came the slightest improvement in the race. And always, at the appointed time, the Swarm returned to its rendezvous among the mountains. Always it returned in vain: there was no messenger from the stars, bringing news of better fortune elsewhere.

As the aeons pass, the Swarm, while immortal, begins to lose its memory, to forget what it is and why it is here. The surface of the Earth undergoes radical transformation during the ice age and the subsequent flooding of the majority of the world's landmass, and yet throughout all of this the species inhabited by the Swarm survives. The Swarm itself is now dissipated, its 'mind' fragmented amongst the thousands of individual members of the species it inhabited millions of years ago,

Only one thing remained – the blind urge which still ... drove it to seek its consummation in a valley that long ago ceased to exist ... Obeying an urge whose meaning they had never known, the doomed legions of the lemmings were finding oblivion beneath the wave.

In a similar scenario, in the 1960 film version of H. G. Wells' *The Time Machine* – although not in the book itself – we see the Eloi continuing to respond to air-raid warning sirens and making their way to the bomb shelters from a long-forgotten war, where the Morlocks are waiting to harvest them.

What is important here is that wherever human beings gather together in a society they imbue their surroundings with special significance, a significance that may persist across numerous generations and become enshrined in tradition, even after the original meaning of the place has been forgotten or has at least faded with age. Birth places and death places, places of sacrifice and glory, as well as those of horror and suffering, are all more than simply 'spaces' to be in. Once again space is not simply a receptacle in which to exist, but it is a context which is intrinsically bonded to human life. Certain public settings serve as extensions of the corporate life of a community. Our personal sense of the sacred is heightened while in a church building, while our appreciation of nature might be accentuated during a walk in the local park. Particular public meeting places, such as parish halls, village greens or the local pub, often heighten our sense of unity with the community. Indeed, the example of the public house is particularly interesting because it does not necessarily have to be 'our local' for it to generate a feeling of comradeship and unity.

War graves and places symbolising human suffering also produce emotional responses within us, even when the events commemorated took place before we were born. It is through our essential relationship with space and place that we maintain our continuity with past generations and with humanity in its widest sense. Many less technologically orientated cultures, such as the Australian aborigines, maintain a far more profound relationship with their landscape than we do in the West: for them each element of the land possesses an important significance. A. Rapoport writes:

Every feature of the landscape is known and has meaning – they then perceive differences which the European cannot see . . . As one example, every individual feature of Ayers Rock is linked to a significant myth and the mythological beings who created it. Every tree, every stain, hole and fissure has meaning. Thus what to a European is an empty land may be full of noticeable differences to the aborigines . . .[18]

We do not simply internalise our feelings and experiences, nor do our actions evaporate the moment after we have performed them, but rather they become part of a total context of internal and external reciprocity. The place where I proposed to my wife is as integral to that experience as are my own personal memories of it. Indeed the weather, the noises, the trees, the buildings and the very time of day were woven together with our words and feelings to form a living and lived-in experience. To be abstracted from that place, or to pretend that the incident took place elsewhere, would beggar the whole experience.

Our whole lives are full of such experiences, not all of them as profound as a proposal of marriage, but they are nevertheless experiences which 'took place'. Indeed it is a cause for much concern that, within developed industrialised countries in particular, a high degree of uniformity of place is being evidenced. Big department stores, airports, fast-food chains, shopping malls, offices and new towns are the same the world over. It is thus becoming increasingly difficult to attach symbolic significance to a particular place when that place fails to express any true particularity.

In connection with this problem of spatial uniformity, it has become quite common within developed countries to hear of the phrase 'architectural space'. By this is meant that space which is 'created' by city and town planners as they seek to utilise society's living space along functional and economic lines. There are two points that must be made concerning this planned or architectural space. First, it involves a conception of space as a neutral and plastic commodity to be manipulated according to purely pragmatic criteria. Secondly, planned space is non-experienced space, it is an abstract and detached space, or what Relph refers to as 'two-dimensional map space',[19] inasmuch as those who have to do with such planning relate to the space involved primarily via maps and blueprints. Thomas Docherty, commenting upon post-war architecture, makes these helpful observations in this regard:

In the wake of the First World War, there were two important determinants of the new style. First urban planning on a large scale was called for as devastated economies tried to rehabilitate themselves; and it was of central importance that cities could be built with a large amount of low-cost materials and standardised units of construction. Secondly, since this first necessity was more or less uniform across Europe, and since

international communications were quickly re-established,
regional or national variations in architectural design began to
disappear. The resulting International Style was characterised
by three central factors. First, design was executed according to
an economy of 'function', according to which the use of a
building was a determinant of style. Secondly, ferroconcrete
and steel, as the main building materials, themselves
determined certain possibilities and limitations in design, such
as geometric regularity. Thirdly, applied decoration was out,
in favour of a kind of austerity. The result was a homogeneity
of urban planning and building design which threatened the
idea of a specific located tradition; in short, the 'genius loci',
the very foundation of architectural thought, was under threat
as a guiding principle for the determination of lived space.[20]

In the film *The Shape of Things to Come*, inspired by the work
of H. G. Wells, much of the technological utopia featured in
the last segment of the film exists underground, a wholly
artificial construct, hewn out of a hillside and artificially lit.
In a scene depicting an elderly man teaching history to his
young granddaughter, we hear of the 'age of windows' when
human beings had to build upwards into the sunlight because
they could not adequately illuminate their world by artificial
means. The response of the enthusiastic little girl is that 'they
keep on inventing things and making the world lovelier and
lovelier'. Of course it is worth noting in passing that for the
most part – the Morlocks and the Selenites, for example – a
subterranean existence is considered by Wells to be rather
dehumanising. In *The Time Machine* Wells goes to great
lengths to explain how the cannibalistic Morlocks are in fact
the ancestors of the poor working classes whose day-to-day
work kept them increasingly underground: 'So, in the end,
above ground you must have the Haves, pursuing pleasure and
comfort and beauty, and below ground the Have-nots; the
Workers getting continually adapted to the conditions of their
labour.'

Whereas the term 'space' properly refers to a broad general

context and setting, the notion of place involves a focusing of our attention and intentions upon a specific location which is at once part of the larger spatial context and yet also stands at a distance from it. The phenomenon of place is not an easy one to define as it manifests itself upon many different and yet interrelated levels, ranging from the broad geographical identification of a land mass to a particular corner of a particular room.

We shall now look at some of the different facets of place, in an attempt to assess the nature of the identity of places. Having done this, we shall move on to the most important issue, as regards this present work – that of our relationship to and experience of place.

The identity of place

In his book *The Myth of Sisyphus*, Albert Camus helpfully identifies three basic elements which need to be included in any discussion concerning the identity of place. These are the physical setting, the activities and the meaning of a place. To these Relph has added a fourth, which he refers to as the spirit of place.[21]

The first of these elements has to do with the distinctive landscape of a place – its topography, overall setting and climate. It is these things to which we immediately respond when encountering a new place. We ask questions such as: Where does this path lead? Where can I park my car? How far away is the sea? We respond to the climate, perhaps thinking it either too hot or too cold; we notice striking features of the landscape such as a cathedral, forest or monument of some sort. All these things play on our senses and allow us to build up a physical picture of the place we are in, which contributes to its overall identity.

While more fantasy than SF, in R. Zelazny's *Amber* chronicles, we are given an interesting insight into the nature of place. They describe how members of the royal family of Amber could transport themselves to any conceivable time and place simply by calling to mind the appearance of that place and, while actually moving, imagining its features appearing one by one, as they continued on their way. By this process they would eventually construct, feature by feature, the required place from their mental picture of it.[22]

Often we seek to identify a place by asking what happens in it. Is it a holiday resort or a financial centre? Is work scarce or plentiful? What takes place in this or that building? In many cases the physical appearance of a structure will provide us with a clue as to the activities that take place within it. Indeed, certain environmental settings act upon us, like custom and tradition, triggering off patterns of behaviour at an unconscious level; for example, being reverent in church and relaxed on the beach.

However, the identity of a place is more than just the sum of its physical appearance and the activities performed within it. The attribution of meaning and significance to a place by a person or group of persons is a vital component in the identity of that place. The experience of a place as my place or as a beautiful place or an awful place may well be founded in its appearance or activities, but that is not to say that they belong to or are inherent in that place. It is we, as human beings, who bestow meaning upon places. We 'name them', we arrange objects in them and we fill them with significance as we live out our lives in them.

The TV series *Babylon 5* begins each episode with a variation on this statement concerning the nature of the eponymous space station:

It was the dawn of the third age of Mankind, ten years after the Earth/Minbari war. The Babylon project was a dream given form. Its goal, to prevent another war by creating a place where humans and aliens could work out their differences peacefully. It's a port of call, a home away from home, for diplomats, hustlers, entrepreneurs and wanderers. Humans and aliens wrapped in two million five hundred thousand tons of spinning metal, all alone in the night. It can be a dangerous place, but it is our last best hope for peace. This is the story of the last of the Babylon stations. The year is 2258, the name of the place is Babylon 5.

Here we have a story which has a place as its central character. The place is defined in terms of its historical location, its purpose, its physical attributes, but also in terms of its symbolic significance and the hopes and expectations attached to it.

There is no one static meaning which can be said to encapsulate the identity of a place for all people and all time. The meanings of a place are as numerous as the people who know it. Consider, for example, the site of Auschwitz or Buchenwald: are they sites of victory for a 'master race' or places of sorrow or shame? Is a public house a place of communal refreshment or a den of iniquity? And are this country's stately homes beautiful pieces of architecture to be preserved, tourist attractions to be marketed, symbols of privilege or a scandalous waste of money and resources?

The relationship between place and humanity

We have separated out from the rest of the elements which make up a place's identity the aforementioned notion of the 'spirit of place'. This is because of the difficulty in addressing this factor in any precise way. A place's 'spirit' or 'atmosphere' may be furnished partly by the three factors discussed above, and yet it remains unchanged despite physical alterations, changes in activity and the attribution of a different meaning to a given place. The spirit of a place is its soul; it is what makes it this place as opposed to any other place in the cosmos. It has to do with the ghosts which haunt a place, long-forgotten people and events which, although historically insignificant in accordance with the prevailing canons of historiography, are nonetheless 'recorded' by their setting, captured and held by their place. Indeed, just as we speak of events 'taking place', so too should we think of places 'taking events'.

Lawrence Durrell sums up this notion of a place's spirit when he writes, somewhat whimsically, of landscapes bestowing their own distinctive character upon those living in them:

I believe you could exterminate the French at one blow and resettle the country with Tartars, and within two generations discover to your astonishment that the national characteristics were back at norm – the restless metaphysical curiosity, the tenderness for good living and the passionate individualism: even though their noses were flat. This is the invisible constant in a place.[23]

This may or may not be so; however, if human beings are indeed such that their identities are intrinsically bound up with their external contexts, then it should in no way surprise us to find evidence of a reciprocal relationship pertaining between humanity and its 'place'. We name places, act in places, fill places with meaning. They, in turn, augment our identities by reflecting them back at us; they help to define our activities and behaviour, they capture the spirits of bygone generations and mediate them to us in the present, thus enriching our lives and enhancing our solidarity with the whole of humankind. Indeed, our looking to various ancient places and our concern to preserve them speaks both of our need to be related to the past but also of our desire that the present be mediated to the future.

In A. E. van Vogt's 1950 short story 'The Enchanted Village' this theme receives an elegant SF treatment. The central character of the story, Bill Jenner, having crash-landed upon the wholly inhospitable planet Mars, discovers a deserted alien village apparently unfavourable to human life. The village's music was painful to his ears, its bathing facilities were toxic to him and the food it produced poisonous. Eventually Jenner comes to the conclusion that the village is actually alive and that it has the ability to adapt itself to the needs of its inhabitants. Much of the story is concerned with Jenner's attempts at trying to get the village to adapt to his needs. However, ultimately it is the man who adapts to his new environment:

'I've won!' thought Jenner, 'the village has found a way!' After a while, he remembered something and crawled to the bathroom. Cautiously, watching the ceiling, he eased himself backward into the shower stall. The yellowish spray came down, cool and delightful. Ecstatically, Jenner wriggled his four-foot tail, and, lifted his long snout to let the thin streams of liquid wash away the food impurities that clung to his sharp teeth. Then he waddled out to bask in the sun, and listen to the timeless music.[24]

As with Woolsey's 'The Star of Double Darkness' – mentioned earlier in this chapter – van Vogt is speaking both of the incredible adaptability of the human species but also of its intimate relationship with its context, its need to be 'in' and 'with'. The human desire to belong to and within a community and setting is often referred to as a need for 'roots'. This botanical image brings to mind the organic relationship that exists between a living entity and its environment. The French writer and philosopher Simone Weil writes, concerning human rootedness:

To be rooted is perhaps the most important and least recognised need of the human soul. It is one of the hardest to define. A human being has roots by virtue of his real, active and natural participation in the life of the community, which preserves in living shape certain particular expectations for the future. This participation is a natural one in the sense that it is automatically brought about by place, conditions of birth, profession and social surroundings. Every human being needs to have multiple roots. It is necessary for him to draw well-nigh the whole of his moral, intellectual and spiritual life by way of the environment of which he forms a part.[25]

This is a theme which is considered at some length in Frank Herbert's epic *Dune* series, where the desert planet of Arrakis is seen to exert a remarkable environmental, physical and spiritual influence upon both its indigenous population, the Fremen, as well as outsiders such as Paul Atreides.[26]

To be rooted is to belong within a place, as well as to a community. 'My place' provides me with a perspective on the rest of the world and allows me to identify myself within that world. As we have mentioned previously, our immediate consciousness of self is extended to incorporate the environment in which we are situated. It is little wonder, therefore, that many people who have had to endure the crisis of having their homes burgled liken the experience to a form of rape.

Harvey Cox refers to a woman from the Czech town of Lidice which was totally effaced by the Nazis. She tells us that, notwithstanding the loss of her family, her most profound shock came when she returned to Lidice to find it no longer existed, not even to the extent of scattered remains and ruined buildings. The woman from Lidice was thus totally displaced, as the setting which formed the matrix of her experience of the past and sense of progression into the future, of her apprehension of human community and activity, and of her sense of belonging within a distinctive identifiable place, ceased to be.

In a similar instance, Isak Dinesen tells us of the Masai tribe of East Africa and the way in which they sought to short-circuit the crisis of displacement, despite the reality of physical relocation: 'The Masai when they were moved from their old country, north of the railway line, to the present reserve, took with them the names of their hills, plains and rivers, and gave them to the hills, plains and rivers in the new country.'[27] This was not a possible option in the case of the woman from Lidice, because her place had 'died' before she was given the chance to effect even a partial transfer of significance from it to a new setting.

In our modern transient society we are constantly forced to relocate for economic and social reasons. We have therefore developed various methods for transferring the significance of 'home' from one locale to another. Thus it is that we seldom, if ever, sell everything we own when we move to a new place, but rather carry with us a vast array of objects which we arrange about us in an attempt to duplicate our previous environment. We take great pleasure in unpacking a favourite picture or a much-loved piece of furniture. And yet, despite our efforts to carry our homes about with us, we are still confronted by the strange streets and unknown buildings which make up our 'new place', and roots, once dug up, need to be re-established. Indeed, in many instances the place that we refer to as 'home' tends to remain home no matter how long we have been absent from it and how far away from it we are geographically.

Television series, such as Irwin Allen's *Lost in Space* (from the 1960s)[28] and *Star Trek: Voyager* (from the 1990s), have as their *raison d'être* the desire to return home, the distracting wonders of the universe notwithstanding. One's home is not simply a house or the place where one happens to live, nor is it a place to which we have a certain degree of attachment. Home is the place where we feel we belong; it is the place that we truly care for and with which we share an almost symbiotic relationship. For example, this sense of possessing a deep and organic bond with a particular place can be found expressed in the Old Testament writings concerning the Hebrews' relationship with the land which God had given them. H. Snyder, drawing on the work of W. Brueggemann, makes the point when he writes:

The Bible is not ... the story of God and his people only, but of God, his people and the land. Land, both as 'actual earthly turf' and as symbol of rootedness or 'historical belonging', ...
is 'a central, if not the central theme of biblical faith'. Keeping the biblical focus on the land before us 'will protect us from excessive spiritualization, so that we recognize that the yearning for land is always a serious historical enterprise concerned with historical power and belonging'.[29]

It should be clear, in the light of our brief discussion of the phenomenon of place, how important this notion is to human identity. Human beings do not simply 'feel' that they ought to be situated but actually *are* situated within real space and real places. Gabriel Marcel has said: 'An individual is not distinct from his place; he is that place.'

It should come as no surprise that a genre such as SF, with its abiding interest in the human condition, be found to be deeply concerned with the notions of place and situation. The genre's fascination with exploration and unknown frontiers, coupled with its concerns over failing resources and over-population, has stimulated an almost trademark interest in colonisation. As we saw in an earlier chapter, Wells' *War of the Worlds* is, in effect, a colonisation story, where a race from a dying world 'regarded this earth with envious eyes' only to be destroyed by the simple fact of being here unprotected from the bacteria that are part of our world.

These germs of disease have taken toll of humanity since the beginning of things – taken toll of our pre-human ancestors since life began here. But by virtue of this natural selection of our kind we have developed resisting-power; to no germ do we succumb without a struggle, and to many – those that cause putrefaction in dead matter, for instance – our living frames are altogether immune. But there are no bacteria in Mars, and directly those invaders arrived, directly they drank and fed, our microscopic allies began to work their overthrow.[30]

The experience of the Martian invaders calls to mind instances within our own history when Napoleon and Hitler both failed to take into account the significance of place and climate when they sought to invade Russia.

Being able to put human beings into new, strange and alien places is clearly part of the attraction of SF. Questions such as 'If place is so important to us, what would happen if we became in some way displaced or if we could radically re-engineer our environment?' rest at the very heart of the genre. We are increasingly aware of the impact our surroundings have upon us, with notions such as 'sick building syndrome' and 'urban renewal' signalling a desire to improve human life via an improvement in the surrounding context. Environmental concerns, in so far as they speak of the need to recognise humanity's intrinsic relationship with its context, are as much exercises in enlightened self-interest as they are expressions of any concern for the non-human world. We have become adept at engineering our environment; we are no longer, in the main, slaves to the earth's rotation about the sun – night and day, summer and winter are all one to us as we live and work in artificially lit, climate-controlled structures.

Yet, our control over our context is less than perfect, our true public spaces appear to be degenerating, becoming dangerous and uninviting, while our private spaces become ever more insulated from the rest of the world. Untold wealth is expended upon creating individually tailored living spaces; interior designers, landscape gardeners, fashion consultants and style gurus appear in TV shows and magazines aimed at maximising our control over our particular spaces, helping us to engineer our ideal private place. In his novel *Snow Crash*, Neal Stephenson envisages a time in which private suburbs – 'burbclaves' – are almost completely isolated from the rest of society as well as other 'burbs'. In the advertising literature seeking to encourage people to take out citizenship in a 'burbclave' known as 'Mr Lee's Greater Hong Kong', it defines itself as 'a private, wholly extraterritorial, sovereign, quasi-national entity . . .'[31]

The phenomenon of the 'theme park' – and to a lesser extent perhaps, the shopping mall – represents an attempt at creating the illusion of public space while in reality these are carefully orchestrated and tightly policed virtual places designed to give the occupant the feeling of being 'out-and-about' while at the same time providing the sense of private security normally associated with being 'indoors'. In many ways these places seem to me to have a great deal in common with Stephenson's 'burbclaves'.

In Michael Crichton's *Westworld* (1973) and subsequently *Jurassic Park* (1990) – both books filmed under the same names – we are confronted with the question: 'What happens when our technologically controlled environments break down?' In both of these stories we are dealing with futuristic theme parks, the first based upon the American wild west, populated by robot cowboys and gunmen, the latter upon the Jurassic period, suitably populated by an array of cloned dinosaurs. While the loss of electrical power is unlikely to result in our being stalked by cybernetic gunmen or *Tyrannosaurus rex*, nevertheless such an occurrence is becoming less and less of a minor inconvenience. Without power we have no lighting, no telecommunications, no heating, our stored food begins to perish as our freezers defrost and we have no access to information. In the worst-case scenario, an instance of a major city-wide blackout, we can expect looting, violence and at least temporary urban chaos. In the months before the change of date from the year 1999 to the year 2000 there was much anxiety that the so-called 'millennium bug' would affect all unmodified computer systems and cause havoc with our virtual places, our information and communication networks, as well as timers on a whole range of 'smart' environmental aids such as heating systems, video recorders, security alarms and personal computers. So far, however, the fear has proved to be unfounded. This of course is the central message of E. M. Forster's anti-Wellesian *The Machine Stops*.[32] It would seem that we are now just as ill-equipped to deal with the natural world, a world without artificial additions, as the *Titanic* and her passengers were to deal with the iceberg and the freezing ocean water.

As societies become more and more privatised and grow increasingly dependent upon the technologies that support such privatisation, there is, it seems to me, an inevitable tendency to look back wistfully to a mythical pastoral age where life was simpler and greener. From the very beginning of the technological revolution there have always been attempts to argue that humanity's natural place is in the organic rather than the artificial world. Rousseau's 'noble savage', epitomised in Edgar Rice Burrough's *Tarzan* as well as Robert E. Howard's *Conan the Barbarian*, speaks of a humanity corrupted by modern culture and technology and idealises a romantic back-to-nature philosophy. Yet, the question needs to be asked: 'What, exactly, is natural for us?' In the latter half of the twentieth century the 'Disneyfication' of the natural world has made every animal our companion, every wild and savage place a potential home, and yet how long would any Western, technologically reared individual survive in a genuinely 'natural' environment, red in tooth and claw? The fantasy writer Terry Pratchett draws our attention to this in his Diskworld novel *Wyrd Sisters*:

Occupying the metterforical [sic] *stalls was a rabble of rabbits, weasels, vermin, badgers, foxes and miscellaneous creatures who, despite the fact that they lived their entire lives in a bloody atmosphere of hunter and hunted, killing or being killed by claw, talon and tooth, are generally referred to as woodland folk.*[33]

To enjoy a walk in the country, to take pleasure in growing things and to appreciate and respect other animals is a far cry from actually living in 'the natural world'. The SF writer Brian Aldiss once made the observation that while he enjoyed the beauty of the trees at the bottom of his garden he had no illusion about their relationship to him – if he stood there long enough the trees would grow through him. The scientist and creator of the Gaia hypothesis, James Lovelock, makes a similar point when he argues:

Gaia, as I see her, is no doting mother tolerant of misdemeanour, nor is she some fragile and delicate damsel in danger from brutal mankind. She is stern and tough, always keeping the world warm and comfortable for those who obey the rules, but ruthless in her destruction of those who transgress. If humans stand in the way of this, we shall be eliminated with as little pity as would be shown by the micro-brain of an intercontinental ballistic nuclear missile in full flight to its target.[34]

While it eventually collapsed into a rather uncritical pastoralism, the BBC series *The Survivors* (1975–77) began by exploring the notion of survival in a post-holocaust, post-technological age. As with the middle segment of the H. G. Wells film *Things to Come*, one of the principle themes of *The Survivors* was how to get the machines started again without petrol. In Richard Matheson's *I Am Legend*, the principle character in this tale of a post-holocaust world adopted the simple expedient of scavenging among the remains of a dead city. In the *Mad Max* series of films, petrol has become a prized commodity that people are prepared to kill for as this substance alone can provide both the power and mobility necessary for survival. Without its machines, technologically acclimatised humanity appears to find it next to impossible to find a place in the so-called natural world: perhaps it is no longer natural to us?

Virtual worlds

In our desire to find or create the perfect place in which to live, the notion of computer-generated 'virtual worlds' has stimulated a considerable degree of interest. The ability to construct an ideal environment personalised to one's own tastes has a certain appeal – particularly when one might have almost godlike control over that world. Currently virtual-reality technology is a long way from presenting us with a convincing world, one that for all its flexibility we would be prepared to actually live in rather than simply be entertained by for an hour or two. Much of what passes for virtual reality at present goes little beyond the familiar boundaries of domestic 3D computer games such as the 'Quake' franchise. In these games one is presented with a first-person perspective view of an invariably hostile environment in which one has the freedom to move and explore as if in a real world. Of course these games are still presented on a TV or monitor and thus, no matter how involved we might become in the game world, we are under no illusion about actually occupying that world. With the invention of VR helmets, which contain small monitors that display images directly in front of our eyes and sensors that alter the display relative to the movement of our heads, the illusion of actual presence in a virtual world is further enhanced. Sensory-feedback gloves and even full body suits have been developed to allow the computer-generated world to 'appear' to be interacting with the human body; nevertheless the illusion is not complete:

'Damn picture postcard,' Pop said to me. 'Beautiful little houses for us to live in, with rose bushes, and ivy on the walls.'

'Well, what's wrong with that?'

'It isn't real. Looks good to you, but I can tell. Not what I remember. Too regular, too clean. There's no grime, no dust, no insects. Just another stage set.'[35]

The notion that we might conceivably be living in an illusory world has its modern roots in the work of the philosopher René Descartes, who argued that while we might be certain of our actual existence we could not, in the first instance, be certain of the location of that existence – everything we seem to be experiencing as physical sensation might turn out to be nothing more than a dream. Descartes' belief in a perfect and benevolent God ultimately provided him with grounds for confidence in the reality of the perceived world, however the suspicion he raised concerning our perception of the world has not gone away.

SF writers have explored the idea of virtual worlds or realities from a variety of perspectives – as entertainment, as therapy, as a means of subjugation and as a strategy for survival.[36] Two key questions which have emerged from the plethora of 'VR' stories are these: 'Is there any reason why one shouldn't choose to live in a virtual world?' and 'Is there an ethic that might be applicable to a virtual world?'

In the main SF has tended to regard virtual worlds as inferior to what we might call the 'real world'. Of course the virtual realities of the future are portrayed as much more convincing than their present-day counterparts, in most cases bypassing the senses altogether and feeding data directly to the brain. In

William Gibson's cyberpunk novels the world's entire data network can be interacted with as if it were a place to visit. By plugging a computer interface directly into a socket in his skull – 'jacking-in' – the central character in *Neuromancer* perceives himself to be occupying 'cyberspace':

Cyberspace. A consensual hallucination experienced daily by billions of legitimate operators, in every nation, by children being taught mathematical concepts . . . A graphic representation of data abstracted from the banks of every computer in the human system. Unthinkable complexity. Lines of light ranged in the nonspace of the mind, clusters and constellations of data. Like city lights, receding . . .[37]

In the comedy SF series *Red Dwarf*, we are introduced to 'Total Immersion Video Games' in the first series episode 'Better Than Life'. The purpose of these games is to provide the user with the perfect illusion of an idyllic world while their actual physical bodies are automatically maintained by intravenous food supplies. In such a world any fantasy can be lived, every pleasure experienced, every taboo broken with no obvious repercussions – in the same way that contemporary computer games such as 'Kingpin' allow players to take on the role of violent criminal gang members without fear of actual arrest and punishment. The obvious outcome of entering such a fantasy world is the strong temptation never to come out again: who, having experienced a world in which they are successful, popular and powerful, would wish to return to a world, no matter how 'real', in which they were a poor, unpopular failure? The potential for VR technology to become for the twenty-first century what chemical drugs have been for the latter part of the twentieth is great indeed. Whether cyber-drugs should elicit the same cause for concern as chemical hallucinogens remains to be debated, although the genre of SF seems, in the main, to be rather suspicious of the technology and its potential for subverting our sense of reality and responsibility.[38]

Of course creating a virtual space might serve no more sinister a purpose than to provide an arena in which individuals, separated by actual physical geography, might congregate and interact in a more realistic way than is possible via telephone, e-mail or chatroom:

Hiro is approaching the Street. It is the Broadway, the Champs-Elysées of the Metaverse . . . it does not really exist. But right now, millions of people are walking up and down it . . . Like any place in Reality, the Street is subject to development. Developers can build their own small streets feeding off the main one. They can build buildings, parks, signs, as well as things that do not exist in Reality . . . The only difference is that the Street does not really exist – it's just a computer-graphics protocol written down on a piece of paper somewhere – none of these things is being physically built. They are, rather, pieces of software, made available to the public over the worldwide fiber-optics network . . . As Hiro approaches the Street, he sees two young couples, probably using their parents' computer for a double date in the Metaverse . . . He is not seeing real people, of course. This is part of the moving illustration drawn by his computer according to specifications coming down the fiber-optics cable. The people are pieces of software called avatars. They are the audiovisual bodies that people use to communicate with each other in the Metaverse. Hiro's avatar is now on the Street, too, and if the couple coming off the monorail look over in his direction, they can see him, just as he's seeing them. They could strike up a conversation: Hiro in the U-Stor-It in L.A. and the four teenagers probably on a couch in a suburb of Chicago . . . [39]

The Enlightenment philosopher Immanuel Kant argued in his *Critique of Pure Reason* that the world we actually live in is, in effect, merely a representation of the real world, the world 'out there' that we can have nothing to do with in itself. When we perceive a table or a person, for example, these actual objects do not occupy our minds as such, what does exist in our minds is the *representation* of these things, images projected into our minds by our senses. If this is indeed the case then perhaps it does not really matter how these images find their way into our minds, via our senses or directly by means of some computer interface with our brains – the end result will still be an image or a representation in the human mind that we can choose to call the *real world*. Philosophers from Plato to Hegel have been unconvinced of the ultimate reality of this physical world, choosing rather to identify some manner of mental, spiritual or metaphysical realm as being truly real, with this world being a transitory or shadow reflection of that reality at best. The Western Christian tradition, having been deeply influenced by Platonism via Augustine, has itself tended towards an other-worldly orientation which regards this present world as in some sense inferior to and less 'real' than some higher spiritual realm. In many ways 'cyberspace' and 'virtual reality' represent a return to the philosophical idealism of Plato, Kant and Hegel, where true reality is acknowledged as being for mind alone.

It would appear that human beings do indeed require location, place and space: we need to be situated, it is part of our self-definition. Where we might choose to be and how we might further engineer environments for ourselves to live in are questions of the highest significance as these issues cut to the very heart of our understanding of what it means to be human. For example, is our principle concern to create environments that best serve the needs and desires of the private individual? Or are we more, or at least equally, concerned with the creation of public spaces, places which encourage human interaction and a sense of communality? Will the inevitable developments in virtual-reality technology encourage increased privatisation, with each individual 'jacked-into' their own perfect private world? Or will it rather spawn the communications utopia envisioned by the likes of Bill Gates, where everyone on the planet become virtual neighbours? Ultimately we occupy places either alone or together and it seems to me that this is one of the most important decisions we need to make as we begin the new millennium.

Conclusion

What have we done?

What I have tried to do throughout this book, with the aid of the genre of science or future fiction, is to bring into focus the human questions that reside at the very centre of our existence. As a species and as individuals we find ourselves cast into unnegotiated existence: like it or not, we are born into a world with a history and as a particular kind of being. In an episode of *Star Trek: The Next Generation* entitled 'The Offspring' the android Data creates a child, another android that finds itself 'activated' – just like Frankenstein's creature – in a strange world full of questions and very few obvious or unambiguous answers. In a conversation with its parent the new android suddenly lets fly with a torrent of existential questions:

LAL: *'Father, what is my purpose?'*
DATA: *'Purpose?'*
LAL: *'My function, my reason for being?'*
DATA: *'That is a complex question, Lal. I can only begin to answer by telling you that our function is to contribute in a positive way to the world in which we live.'*
LAL: *'Why am I me instead of someone else?'*
DATA: *'Because you are my child.'*
LAL: *'Where did I come from? . . . Why do we have two hands? Why not three or four? Why is the sky black? Why do . . .?'*

At this point Data, overwhelmed by his child's metaphysical and epistemological questions, switches her off for the night.

It is these questions and others like them that have concerned us here – questions concerning what it might mean to be human and how we might conduct ourselves as human beings in this world in which we find ourselves. These are fundamental religious and philosophical questions and ones that ought, at some level, to engage us all. I say at some level because it is clearly the case that some are better suited by training or inclination to tackle these issues directly via the traditional academic disciplines, while others find such debates too rarefied, the language used too impenetrable and the background history of ideas too labyrinthine to relate to confidently or comfortably. Nevertheless, these debates are important to us all and it is my conviction that they might usefully be engaged with by means other than those traditional to academic study. Literature and the media, in all their forms, can provide us with valuable stimuli for discussion and debate on a variety of topics. While countless individuals all over the world might read a best-selling novel or watch a particular film, there are relatively few who will ever read the works of Plato, Descartes, Hegel or Levinas. Stimulus for reflection upon who we are and what our purpose might be is very much where we find it. I have looked here within a genre that I have always found to be both intellectually valuable and personally entertaining – that of future fiction.

What have we not done?

Some readers will have reached the end of this book and, whatever they might think of its merits or lack of them, may find themselves wondering about the promised religious component to the work. The book does, after all, bear the subtitle 'Religious Themes in Science Fiction': so where are these religious themes? In answer to this question I have two points to make in the book's defence. First of all, the subtitle is 'Religious *Themes* in Science Fiction', and not simply 'Religion in Science Fiction'; the focus of attention has not been upon religions as such but rather on some of the themes that I consider central to religions. In planning this work I wanted to avoid falling into the trap of 'religion spotting', simply cataloguing and commenting on the various religions and religious practices depicted within the genre of SF. While such a work may well have proved interesting at some level, it strikes me as a singularly unhelpful exercise for those who would seek to explore the nature of the questions religions concern themselves with. A study of this kind would simply provide us with an insight into the varieties of different religious traditions and a list of where they occur within the genre of SF and this was not my intention for this work.

The second point I wish to make draws upon a profound observation made by the Christian theologian Wolfhart Pannenberg, who makes this point with respect to the conflict between religion and atheism:

The basic question posed by modern atheism is this: Does man, in the exercise of his existence, assume a reality beyond himself and everything finite, sustaining him in the very act of his freedom, and alone making him free, a reality to which everything that is said about God refers? Or does the freedom of man exclude the existence of God . . .?[1]

Any choice between a religious or an atheistic perspective upon human existence is, argues Pannenberg, ultimately a choice between distinct anthropologies, between ways of understanding the human condition. What I have tried to do here is to make use of a particular literary genre as a means of stimulating an exploration into this primary religious theme of human being. Theologians such as Friedrich Schleiermacher in the nineteenth century and Wolfhart Pannenberg in the twentieth have argued that the human question is best answered in a religious mode, that human being makes best sense from a religious perspective, with humanity understood as dependent upon or open to that which transcends it. To argue such a case for the significance of the religious response to the human question requires a familiarity with the contours of the question – What are we? Where are we going? Where do we belong? – as well as with the range of possible answers.

I believe that the genre of SF has had this question and its various answers at its very heart, ever since Frankenstein's creature first drew breath, and I hope that this current work both reflects this and further serves to stimulate reflection upon the question.

Notes

PREFACE
1. R. Scholes, *Structural Fabulation* (University of Notre Dame Press, 1975), pp.29–30.

CHAPTER 1: 'Aliens and Androids and Cyborgs, Oh My!'
1. For example, Brian Aldiss, *Billion Year Spree* (Corgi, 1975); J. Clute & P. Nicholls (eds), *The Encyclopedia of Science Fiction* (St Martin's Press, 1995).
2. The most recent being S. May, *Star Dust and Ashes: Science Fiction in Christian Perspective* (SPCK, 1998).
3. ST: DS9, 'The Emissary'.
4. John Calvin, *Institutes of the Christian Religion*, ed. J. T McNeill (Westminster, 1960), p. 35.
5. Aldiss, *Billion Year Spree*, p.3.
6. T. S. Kuhn, *The Structure of Scientific Revolutions*, 1964.
7. F. Bacon, in his biography of Henry VII, cited in N. Hampson, *The Enlightenment* (Penguin, 1987), p.36.
8. F. Bacon, *Novum Organum* Bk 2.
9. Cf. Laplace's famous conversation with Napoleon.
10. Cf. Locke's two 'Treatises on Government'.
11. L. W. Beck, 'What have we learned from Kant?' in *Self and Nature in Kant's Philosophy*, ed. A. Wood (Cornell University Press, 1984) p.28.
12. Kant, *Critique of Pure Reason*, A125–126.
13. Ibid. A126.
14. Aldiss, *Billion Year Spree*, p.1.
15. Scholes, *Structural Fabulation*, pp.41–42.
16. H. Gernsback, *Wonder Stories* (Stellar Publishing Corp., 1932).
17. A. C. Clarke, 'The Third Law' in *Profiles of the Future* (1962, republished Gollancz, 1999).
18. W. Pannenberg, *Anthropology in Theological Perspective* (T & T Clarke, 1985) p.45.
19. W. Pannenberg, *Jesus, God and Man* (SCM, 1968) p.206.

CHAPTER 2: The Primal Question: What Are We?
1. STNG, 'The Measure of a Man'.
2. P. Cadigan, *Fools* (HarperCollins, 1994).
3. R. Descartes, *Discourse on Method 4* (Penguin Classics, 1976), p.53.
4. Ibid. p.54.
5. Aldiss, *Billion Year Spree*, p.280.

6. Cf. J. Hick, *Evil and the God of Love* (Macmillan, 1966).
7. D. Gerrold, *The Man Who Folded Himself* (Bantam, 1991), p.66.
8. Schleiermacher, *The Christian Faith* (T & T Clark, 1928).
9. Karl Barth, *Church Dogmatics*, vol. 3/2 (T & T Clark, 1958–60), p.250.
10. Ibid. p.227.
11. W. Pannenberg, *Human Nature, Election and History*, (Westminster, 1972), p.26.
12. Cf. E. Levinas, *Totality and Infinity* (The Hague: Martinus Nijhoff, 1979).
13. Mary Shelley, *Frankenstein or The Modern Prometheus* (OUP, 1992) p.100.
14. J. Moltman, *God in Creation*, p.4.

CHAPTER 3: Aliens We

1. *The Invisible Enemy* (BBC, 1977).
2. 'Anthropology' in Clute & Nicholls, *The Encyclopedia of Science Fiction*.
3. H. G. Wells, *The War of the Worlds* (Pan, 1978) p.9.
4. Cf. *The Shape of Things to Come*.
5. *The War of the Worlds*, p.11.
6. Ibid. p.106ff. cf. p.112.
7. In 1938 a radio play by Orson Welles based on *The War of the Worlds* was mistaken for a real alien invasion and caused widespread panic in the US.
8. Cf. A. West, *Deadly Innocence* (Mowbray, 1995) and N. Noddings, *Women and Evil* (University of California Press, 1989) for a more theological treatment of this theme.
9. *Frankenstein*, p.53.
10. Ibid. p.57.
11. *The War of the Worlds*, p.25.
12. Cf. *Frankenstein*, p.58.
13. *Babylon 5*, J. M. Straczynski, 'Infection' (Warner Home Video, 1993).
14. Cf. The Sermon on the Mount (Matt. 5–7).
15. STNG, 'The Best of Both Worlds', Pt 2 (CIC videos, 1990).
16. George Orwell, *Nineteen Eighty-Four* (Penguin Books, 1972) p.208.
17. STNG, 'I-Borg' (CIC videos, 1992).
18. In a later story, 'Decent', we learn that, ironically, this Borg's new sense of individuality 'infects' the Borg collective, causing a number of them to abandon the collective.
19. Cf. *Star Trek: Voyager* and its introduction of the Borg character, 7 of 9.
20. J. Gunn, *The Road to Science Fiction*, vol.5: *The British Way* (White Wolf Publishing, 1998), p.14.
21. Cf. D. Thomson, *The Alien Quartet* (Bloomsbury, 1998) for an interesting treatment of the four films.
22. I. Kant, *Groundwork of the Metaphysics of Morals* (Hutchinson, 1969), p.91.
23. Ibid. p.97.
24. Ibid. p.95.
25. Ibid. p.91, cf. p.95f.
26. M. Alsford, 'Post-Modern Deconstruction of Self in Atonement' in *Atonement Today*, p.214ff.
27. *Social Trends* 18, 1988, p.36f.

28. J. H. Goldthorpe and D. Lockwood, *The Affluent Worker in the Class Structure* (CUP, 1969), p.96–97.
29. A. Britten, *The Privatized World*, p.49.
30. M. Pawley, *The Private Future* (Thames & Hudson, 1973), p.8.
31. Ibid. p.11.
32. It is interesting to note the recent attempt by the computer entertainment industry to create an image of sociality with respect to video gaming. The proliferation of 'online' games and the inclusion of modems within both Sega's Dreamcast and Sony's Playstation 2 are highly significant in this regard.
33. Pawley, p.46.
34. Ibid. p.100.
35. Cf K. Busiek & A. Ross, *Marvels* (Marvel Comics, 1999) – a fascinating graphic novel that traces the emergence of the first superheroes into the world from the point of view of ordinary people.
36. E. Levinas in conversation with R. Kearney in *Dialogues with Contemporary Continental Thinkers* (MUP, 1984) p.60.
37. Ibid. p.60.
38. *The Day the Earth Stood Still* (20th Century Fox, 1951).
39. R. B. Pippin, *Modernism as a Philosophical Problem* (Blackwell, 1991) pp.91–92.
40. Jean-François Lyotard, *The Postmodern Condition: A Report on Knowledge* (MUP, 1991) p.xxiv.

CHAPTER 4: Where Are We Going and How Do We Get There?

1. Søren Kierkegaard, *The Journals*, 1 August 1835.
2. The philosopher David Hume makes this point when he argues that so-called natural laws such as cause and effect cannot be demonstrated to be universal and yet we must live as if they were.
3. R. Matheson, *I Am Legend* (Orion, 1999), p.12.
4. Ibid. p.160.
5. Karl Barth, *Church Dogmatics*, vol. 1/1, p.238.
6. G. Zebrowski, 'This Life and Later Ones' in *Simulations*, ed. Karie Jacobson (Citadel Press, 1993).
7. Ibid. p.140.
8. Ibid. p.141.
9. Ibid. p.146–147.
10. This is a a theme previously developed in the film *Forbidden Planet*, in which we learn of a race of super-beings who wipe themselves out when the monsters from their subconscious utilise their power to create by pure thought.
11. Zebrowski, p.150.
12. Geoffrey Robertson, *Crimes Against Humanity: The Struggle for Global Justice* (Penguin, 1999), p.xiii.
13. Ibid. p.12.
14. Ibid. p.21.
15. Ibid. p.23.
16. Ibid. p.24.
17. C. S. Lewis, *Voyage to Venus* (Pan, 1953), pp.111–112.
18. Voltaire, *Candide, or Optimism* (Penguin, 1947).
19. Plato, *The Republic*, 433a.
20. *Star Trek: The Next Generation*, 'The Masterpiece Society'.
21. Augustine, *City of God*, V.17.

22. J. Carey (ed.) *The Faber Book of Utopias* (Faber, 1999), p.xi.
23. S. Firestone, *The Dialectic of Sex: The Case for Feminist Revolution* (Jonathan Cape, 1971).
24. Sally Miller Gearhart, *The Wonderground: Stories of the Hill Women* (Women's Press, 1985), p.3.
25. Cf. Chapter 1 page 19.
26. Cf. F. Manuel (ed.), *Utopias and Utopian Thought* (Souvenir Press, 1973).
27. Sometimes retitled as *The Stars My Destination* (1957).
28. J. Clute & P. Nicholls (eds), *The Encyclopedia of Science Fiction* (St Martin's Press, 1995).
29. H. Ellison, 'I Have No Mouth, and I Must Scream' (1967), reprinted in *The SF Collection* (Chancellor Press, 1994), p.368–369.
30. 'The Atonement and the Post-Modern Deconstruction of the Self' in J. Goldingay (ed.) *Atonement Today* (SPCK, 1995).

CHAPTER 5: Where Do We Belong?

1. Levinas, *Totality and Infinity*, p.152ff.
2. M. Polanyi, *Personal Knowledge*, p.55ff.
3. M. Merleau-Ponty, *Phenomenology of Perception*, pp.100–101.
4. M. Midgley, 'Towards a New Understanding of Human Nature: The Limits of Individualism', in D. J. Ortner (ed.), *How Humans Adapt: A Biocultural Odyssey* (Smithsonian Press, 1983), p.522.
5. In T. Shippey (ed.) *The Oxford Book of Science Fiction Stories* (OUP, 1992) pp.115–126.
6. A similar theme is explored in Gregory Benford's 1995 short story 'Immersion' in *The Best New SF 10*, ed. G. Dozois (Raven Books, 1997), pp.1–52, where a human mind is electronically transferred into the body of a chimp.
7. M. Merleau-Ponty, *Visible and Invisible*, p.117.
8. Ibid. p.115.
9. Polanyi, *Personal Knowledge*, p.59.
10. Merleau-Ponty, *Phenomenology of Perception*, p.143.
11. Cf. G. Zebrowski, 'This Life and Later Ones', (1987) in *Simulations*, ed. K. Jacobson (Citadel Press, 1993). This story is discussed here in Chapter 4.
12. E. Relph, *Place and Placelessness* (Pion, 1976), p.1.
13. Gamel Woolsey, 'The Star of Double Darkness', *Saturday Evening Post*, 18 June 1955. Reprinted with commentary by M. Alsford in *The Powys Journal*, vol. VIII, 1998, ed. J. R. Williams.
14. M. Alsford, 'The Star of Double Darkness by Gamel Woolsey', *The Powys Journal*, vol. VIII, 1998, p.160.
15. Relph, *Place and Placelessness*, pp.9–10.
16. J. G. Ballard, *Billennium* (1961), reprinted in T. Shippey (ed.) *The Oxford Book of Science Fiction Stories* (OUP, 1992), pp.289–290.
17. Relph, *Place and Placelessness*, p.12.
18. A. Rapoport, 'Australian Aborigines and the Definition of Place', in *Environmental Design*, ed. W. J. Mitchell, vol.1 (Los Angeles, 1972), pp.14–15.
19. Cf. Relph, pp.27f.
20. T. Docherty (ed.) *Postmodernism: A Reader* (Harvester Wheatsheaf, 1993), p.265.

21. A. Camus, *The Myth of Sisyphus* (Vintage Books, 1955), pp.130–131. Cf. Relph, pp.46ff.
22. Cf. R. Zelazny, *Nine Princes in Amber* (Faber, 1972).
23. Cf. Relph, p.30.
24. A. E. van Vogt, 'The Enchanted Village' (1950), republished in D. G. Hartwell (ed.) *The Science Fiction Century* (Quality Paperback, 1997).
25. Cited in Relph, p.40.
26. Cf. F. Herbert, *Dune* (1965) as well as its many sequels.
27. *Out of Africa*, cited in Lynch, *What Time Is This Place?* (MIT Press, 1972), p.41.
28. In fact most of Allen's output from the 1960s had the desire to return home as a central motif. Cf. *The Time Tunnel* (1966–67) and *Land of The Giants* (1968–70).
29. H. Snyder, *Liberating the Church* (Marshall, Morgan & Scott, 1983), p.46. Cf W. Brueggemann, *The Land* (Fortress Press, 1977).
30. Wells, *The War of the Worlds*, p.180.
31. N. Stephenson, *Snow Crash* (ROC, 1993), p.92.
32. E. M. Forster, 'The Machine Stops' (1928), in Hartwell, *The Science Fiction Century*, pp.139–160.
33. Terry Pratchett, *Wyrd Sisters* (Corgi, 1989), p.78.
34. J. Lovelock, *The Ages of Gaia* (OUP, 1989), p.212.
35. Zebrowski, *This life and Later Ones*, in *Simulations*, pp.148–149.
36. Cf. The 'Holodecks' in the *Star Trek* series (1980s and 1990s). The 1999 film *The Matrix* and Philip K. Dick's novel *A Maze of Death* (1970), in which the crew of a stranded spaceship keep themselves sane by entering virtual worlds.
37. W. Gibson, *Neuromancer* (Grafton, 1988), p.67.
38. One of the best examples of VR as drug is to be found in Jeff Noon's *Vurt* (Pan, 1993) and its sequel *Pollen* (Ringpull, 1995).
39. Stephenson, *Snow Crash*, pp.23–24, 33.

CONCLUSION

1. W. Pannenberg, *Basic Questions in Theology*, vol.3 (SCM, 1971), p.87ff.

Further Reading

All publishing details and dates refer to the texts used by the author and do not necessarily reflect original dates of publication.

Selected SF reference and critical works:

B. Aldiss, *Billion Year Spree*, Corgi, 1975
B. Aldiss and D. Wingrove, *Trillion Year Spree*, Gollancz, 1986
K. Amis, *New Maps of Hell: a Survey of Science Fiction*, Gollancz, 1961
M. Altman and D. Solter, *Exploring Deep Space and Beyond*, Boxtree, 1993
L. Armitt (ed.) *Where No Man Has Gone Before: Women and Science Fiction*, Routledge, 1991
L. Armitt, *Theorising the Fantastic*, Arnold, 1996
I. Asimov, *Asimov of Science Fiction*, Doubleday, 1981
I. Asimov, *Asimov's Galaxy: Reflections on Science Fiction*, Doubleday, 1989
J. Brosnan, *The Primal Screen: A History of Science Fiction Film*, Orbit, 1991
J. Clute and P. Nicholls, *The Encyclopedia of Science Fiction*, St Martin's Press, 1995
R. Fulton, *The Encyclopedia of TV Science Fiction*, Boxtree, 1995
U. Le Guin, *The Language of the Night*, Women's Press, 1989
P. Hardy (ed.), *The Aurum Film Encyclopedia: Science Fiction*, Aurum Press, 1991
R. Holdstock (ed.), *Encyclopedia of Science Fiction*, Octopus Books, 1978
S. Lefanu, *In the Chinks of the World Machine: Feminism and Science Fiction*, Women's Press, 1988
S. May, *Star Dust and Ashes: Science Fiction in Christian Perspective*, SPCK, 1998
P. Parrinder, *Science Fiction, Its Criticism and Teaching*, Methuen, 1980
D. Pringle, *The Ultimate Guide to Science Fiction*, Grafton, 1990
R. Scholes, *Structural Fabulation*, University of Notre Dame Press, 1975
D. Suvin, *Positions and Presuppositions in Science Fiction*, Macmillan, 1988
D. Thomson, *The Alien Quartet*, Bloomsbury, 1998
D. Wingrove (ed.) *The Source Book of Science Fiction*, Van Nostrand Reinhold, 1984

Selected SF reading
There is a wealth of good SF reading available from mainstream bookshops and local libraries. Here are some suggestions to get you started.

General anthologies
E. Brosnan (comp.), *The SF Collection*, Chancellor Press, 1994
G. Dozois (ed.), *The Best New SF* (published annually), Raven Books
James Gunn (ed.), *The Road to Science Fiction*, vols 1–5, Borealis (an imprint of White Wolf Publishing)
D. G. Hartwell (ed.), *The Science Fiction Century*, Quality Paperback Book Club, 1997
K. Jacobson (ed.), *Simulations: 15 Tales of Virtual Reality*, Citadel Press, 1993
T. Shippey, *The Oxford Book of Science Fiction*, OUP, 1992
B. Stirling, *Mirror Shades*, Ace Books, 1988

Novels and collected works
(ss signifies short story collection)
Isaac Asimov, *Foundation*, Panther, 1975
Isaac Asimov, (ss) *I, Robot*, Panther, 1974
Ian M. Banks, *The Player of Games*, Orbit, 1989
A. Bester, *The Stars My Destination*, Vintage Books, 1996
A. Bester, *The Demoloished Man*, Vintage Books, 1996
K. Busiek and A. Ross, *Marvels*, Marvel Comics, 1999 (a graphic novel)
P. Chadwick, *The Death Guard*, ROC, 1992
A. C. Clarke, (ss) *Reach For Tomorrow*, Corgi, 1974
P. K. Dick, *A Maze of Death*, Pan, 1970
P. José Farmer, (ss) *The Book of Philip José Farmer*, Granada, 1983
D. Gerrold, *The Man Who Folded Himself*, Bantam, 1991
W. Gibson, *Burning Chrome*, Grafton, 1988
U. Le Guin, *The Dispossessed*, Panther, 1974
U. Le Guin, *The Left Hand of Darkness*, Futura, 1981
P. Hamilton, *The Reality Dysfunction*, Pan, 1996
R. A. Heinlein, *Stranger in a Strange Land*, New English Library, 1980
F. Herbert, *Dune*, Gollancz, 1965.
C. S. Lewis, *Out of the Silent Planet*, Pan, 1977
C. S. Lewis, *Voyage to Venus*, Pan, 1976
C. S. Lewis, *That Hideous Strength*, Pan, 1977
R. Matheson, *I Am Legend*, Orion Books, 1999
S. Miller Gearhart, *The Wanderground: Stories of the Hill Women*, Women's Press, 1979
G. Orwell, *Nineteen Eighty-Four*, Penguin, 1972
T. Pratchett, *Wyrd Sisters*, Corgi, 1988
Kim Stanley Robinson, *Red Mars*, HarperCollins, 1993
J. Russ, *The Female Man*, Women's Press, 1985
M. Shelley, *Frankenstein*, OUP, 1992
Cordwainer Smith, *The Rediscovery of Man*, Orion Books, 1999
A. E. van Vogt, (ss) *The Gryb*, New English Library, 1980
A. E. van Vogt, *Slan*, Panther, 1974
A. E. van Vogt, (ss) *More than Superhuman*, New English Library, 1975
H. G. Wells, *The War of the Worlds*, Pan, 1975

Cyberpunk
J. Brunner, *The Shockwave Rider*, Ballantine Books, 1976
P. Cadigan, *Fools*, HarperCollins, 1994
W. Gibson, *Neuromancer*, Grafton, 1986
W. Gibson, *Count Zero*, Grafton
W. Gibson, *Mona Lisa Overdrive*, Grafton

J. Noon, *Vurt*, Pan, 1993
J. Noon, *Pollen*, Ringpull, 1995
N. Stephenson, *Snow Crash*, ROC, 1992
J. Womack, *Terraplane*, Grafton
J. Womack, *Heathen*, Grafton, 1991

Academic works

M. Alsford, 'The Star of Double Darkness by Gamel Woolsey' in *The Powys Journal*, vol. VIII, 1998, ed. J. Williams
Augustine, *City of God*, ed. H. Bettenson (Penguin, 1984)
K. Barth, *Church Dogmatics*, trans. and ed., G. W. Bromiley and T. F. Torrance, T and T. Clark. Vols. 1:1, 1936; 2:1, 1957; 3:1,2,3, 1958–60; 4:1, 1956
L. W. Beck, 'What have we learned from Kant?' in *Self and Nature in Kant's Philosophy*, ed. A.Wood, Cornell University Press, 1984
A. Britten, *The Privatized World*, Routledge & Kegan Paul, 1977
W. Brueggemann, *The Land*, Fortress Press, 1977
A. Camus, *The Myth of Sisyphus*, Vintage Books, 1955
J. Carey (ed.) *The Faber Book of Utopias*, Faber, 1999
J. Calvin, *Institutes of the Christian Religion*, ed. J. T. McNeill, Westminster Press, 1960
R. Descartes, *Discourse on Method: Discourse 4*, Penguin Classics, 1976
S. Connor *Postmodern Culture*, Blackwell, 1994
T. Docherty (ed.), *Postmodernism: A Reader*, Harvester Wheatsheaf, 1993
S. Firestone, *The Dialectic of Sex: The Case for Feminist Revolution*, Jonathan Cape, 1971
J. Goldingay (ed.), *Atonement Today*, SPCK, 1995
J. H. Goldthorpe and D. Lockwood, *The Affluent Worker in the Class Structure*, CUP, 1969
J. Hick, *Evil and the God of Love*, Macmillan, 1966
Immanuel Kant, *Critique of Pure Reason*, trans. Norman Kemp Smith, Macmillan, 1982
R. Kearney, *Dialogue with Contemporary Continental Thinkers*, MUP, 1984
T. S. Kuhn, *The Structure of Scientific Revolutions*, 1964
E. Levinas, *Totality and Infinity*, Martinus Nijhoff, 1979
J. Lovelock, *The Ages of Gaia*, OUP, 1989
Jean-François Lyotard, *The Postmodern Condition: A Report on Knowledge*, MUP, 1991
F. Manuel (ed.), *Utopias and Utopian Thought*, Souvenir Press, 1973
M. Merleau-Ponty, *Phenomenology of Perception*, Routledge, 1962
M. Merleau-Ponty, *Visible and Invisible*, Northwestern University Press, 1968.
M. Midgley, 'Towards a New Understanding of Human Nature: The Limits of Individualism', in *How Humans Adapt: A Biocultural Odyssey*, ed. D. J. Ortner, Smithsonian Press, 1983
J. Moltman, *God in Creation*, SCM, 1985
N. Noddings, *Women and Evil*, University of California Press, 1989
W. Pannenberg, *Anthropology in Theological Perspective*, T. & T. Clark, 1985
W. Pannenberg, *Jesus, God and Man*, SCM, 1968
W. Pannenberg, *Basic Questions in Theology*, vol. 3, SCM, 1971
M. Pawley, *The Private Future*, Thames & Hudson, 1973
R. B. Pippin, *Modernism as a Philosophical Problem*, Blackwell, 1991

Plato, *The Republic*, Penguin, 1977

M. Polanyi, *Personal Knowledge: Towards a Post-Critical Philosophy*, Routledge & Kegan Paul, 1958

A. Rapoport, 'Australian Aborigines and the Definition of Place' in *Environmental Design*, ed. W. J. Mitchell, vol. 1, Los Angeles, 1972

E. Relph, *Place and Placelessness*, Pion Ltd, 1976

G. Robertson, *Crimes Against Humanity*, Penguin, 1999

N. Rose, *Governing the Soul: The Shaping of the Private Self*, Routledge, 1990

F. Schleiermacher, *The Christian Faith*, T. & T. Clark, 1928

H. Snyder, *Liberating the Church*, Marshall, Morgan & Scott, 1983

A. Synnott, *The Body Social: Symbolism, Self and Society*, Routledge, 1993

Voltaire, *Candide, or Optimism*, Penguin, 1947

A. West, *Deadly Innocence*, Mowbray, 1995

Miscellaneous

There are a number of very useful SF magazines and web-sites, some based in the UK and some in the US. The following list is just a sample.

Starlog   Probably the best, and also the best known, of the US-based SF monthly magazines; also available in the UK from specialist shops and some newsagents. Full of news articles and reviews of all things SF. Web-site: www.starlog.com

SFX   The best all-round SF magazine in the UK. Contains news, TV listings, reviews and articles. Web-site: www.sfx.co.uk

TV Zone   A long-running UK magazine that specialises in TV sci-fi.

What If? web-site   This is a web-site designed to support this book, providing further information on SF texts, films and study resources, plus questions for group discussion and links to other sites. www.gre.ac.uk/am03/whatif

www.scifi.com   This is an excellent and constantly updated SF web-site that contains information on all that is new in the genre.

www.uiowa.edu/sfs   A valuable academic SF site containing a number of useful articles on a range of SF themes.

Selected Television and Film Science Fiction

Television

See R. Fulton, *The Encyclopedia of TV Science Fiction*, Boxtree, 1995.

Star Trek Most, but certainly not all, of the series and its spin-offs (*Star Trek: the Next Generation*, *Deep Space Nine* and *Voyager*) repay viewing. They project an enlightened humanistic future, humanity come of age among the stars. Easy viewing, readily available on video, constantly shown and reshown on TV.

Babylon 5 In my view one of the best pieces of SF TV. Far less optimistic about humanity, heroic and bleak by turns. A sustained five-year story arc. Available on video and repeated on a number of channels.

Dr Who Classic long-running (mid-1960s to early 1990s) BBC series now, alas, cancelled. Alien time lord with a love of Earth travels through space and time battling evil. Highly moral, sometimes quite thought-provoking. Made on a very limited budget. A number of videos available.

Red Dwarf Comedy SF series with some very interesting themes – fun and stimulating. Available on video, repeated regularly.

Sliders Group of young Americans travel between parallel dimensions. Quite a good series, plenty to think about. Takes the 'what if' approach to SF: what if the Nazis won the war, the Lottery were a matter of life or death, the world were to end tomorrow, etc.

Stargate SG1 Based on the film of the same name. Aliens posing as ancient gods return to earth through the eponymous stargate only to find that we are not so easily fooled any more. The series has a small semi-military team (SG1) travelling to the 'world of the week' in an effort to find the alien's home world and defeat them. New worlds, new people, new customs/cultures.

The X-Files Difficult to categorise, perhaps not really SF. Two FBI agents investigate strange and bizarre phenomena – one agent is a believer, the other a scientific sceptic.

Lexx Self-parody of the SF genre, sometimes referred to as 'Star Trek's dark twin'.

Total Recall 2070 A cyberpunk series loosely based on the films *Total*

Recall and *Blade Runner*. Artificial life and virtual reality are the key themes here.

Films

See J. Brosnan, *The Primal Screen: A History of Science Fiction Film*, Orbit, 1991.

Frankenstein, 1931 (the Karloff, James Whale version)
Bride of Frankenstein, 1935 (finishes off the original story)
The Invisible Man, 1933 (based on H. G. Wells' book)
Things to Come, 1936 (based on H. G. Wells' book)
The Day the Earth Stood Still, 1951 (classic messianic SF)
The Thing from Another World, 1951 (remade in the 1980s as *The Thing*)
When Worlds Collide, 1951 (rather good end-of-the-world/Noah's Ark in space story)
Invaders from Mars, 1953 (cold war, reds under the bed SF)
Them!, 1954 (giant ant movie, a must see!)
This Island Earth, 1954
Invasion of the Body Snatchers, 1955 (the definitive fear-of-communism SF movie)
Forbidden Planet, 1958 (absolute classic, based on *The Tempest*, apparently)
The Time Machine, 1960 (based on H. G. Wells' book)
2001, A Space Odyssey, 1968
Planet of the Apes, 1968 (alternative-reality/post-apocalypse movie)
The Andromeda Strain, 1971 (biological disaster movie)
Solaris, 1972 (often referred to as the Russian 2001)
Westworld, 1973 (amusement park of the future goes wrong)
Dark Star, 1974 (Hippies in space)
Silent Running (1970s environmental movie)
Phase IV, 1974 (ants, but not giant ones this time, attack humanity)
Logan's Run, 1976
Mad Max 1,2 & 3, 1979–85 (post-apocalypse series of movies)
Alien, 1979, *Aliens*, 1986, *Alien 3*, 1992, *Alien Resurrection*, 1997
Nineteen Eighty-Four (based on George Orwell's book of the same name)
The Terminator, 1984 (time travel, man and machine movie)
Robocop, 1987 (man/machine/identity movie)
AKIRA, 1987 (the Manga movie)
Blade Runner, 1989 (classic cyberpunk film)
The Fly, 1989 (man turns into giant fly!)
Total Recall, 1990 (memories and identity movie)
Delicatessen, 1991
The City of Lost Children, 1991
Terminator 2: Judgment Day, 1992
Twelve Monkeys, 1995 (excellent time-travel/insanity movie)
Star Trek: First Contact, 1996 (see some of the series first or this won't make much sense)
Mars Attacks!, 1997 (great piece of post-modern SF)
Contact, 1997 (interesting treatment of the nature of belief)
The Matrix, 1999 (excellent virtual-reality film)

Index